BELIEF IN SCIENCE
AND
IN CHRISTIAN LIFE

The Relevance of Michael Polanyi's
Thought for Christian Faith
and Life

To

MAGDA POLANYI

in appreciation and affection

BELIEF IN SCIENCE
AND
IN CHRISTIAN LIFE:

The Relevance of Michael Polanyi's Thought for Christian Faith and Life

Editor

THOMAS F. TORRANCE

ST. JOSEPH'S UNIVERSITY   STX

BL240.2.B43
Belief in science and in Christian life

3 9353 00103 2133

BL
240.2
.B43

1980

THE HANDSEL PRESS
EDINBURGH

192473

Published by
The Handsel Press Ltd.
33 Montgomery Street, Edinburgh

ISBN 0 905312 11 2

First published 1980

1980 © T. F. Torrance

All rights reserved. No part of this publication may be reproduced,
stored in retrieval system, or transmitted, in any form, or by any means,
electronic, mechanical, photocopying, recording or otherwise, without
the prior permission of The Handsel Press Ltd.

Printed in Great Britain by
Clark Constable Ltd., Edinburgh

CONTENTS

ACKNOWLEDGMENTS

Grateful acknowledgment is made to the following publishers for permission to cite so freely from Michael Polanyi's works:

Routledge and Kegan Paul
University of Chicago Press
Oxford University Press
International Universities Press

Principal Works of Michael Polanyi
to which reference is made

Science, Faith and Society, University of Chicago Press, Phoenix edition, 1964. First published by Oxford University Press, 1946

The Logic of Liberty, Routledge and Kegan Paul, 1951

Personal Knowledge. Towards a Post-Critical Philosophy, Routledge and Kegan Paul, 1958

The Study of Man, Routledge and Kegan Paul, 1959

The Tacit Dimension, Routledge and Kegan Paul, 1967

Knowing and Being. Essays by Michael Polanyi, edited by Marjorie Grene. Routledge and Kegan Paul, 1969

Scientific Thought and Social Reality. Essays by Michael Polanyi, edited by Fred Schwarz. *Psychological Issues*, vol. VIII/Number 4. Monograph 32. International Universities Press, 1974

Meaning (with Harry Prosch), University of Chicago Press, 1975

MICHAEL POLANYI

AN APPRECIATION

WALTER JAMES
Principal, St. Catherine's, Cumberland Lodge

I first came to know the Polanyis and Michael in 1937, when he was the distinguished Professor of Physical Chemistry at the University of Manchester. His son John was a boy at Manchester Grammar School.

The University supplied illustrious company for him. P. M. S. Blackett was Professor of Physics, and he and his wife were close friends of the Polanyis, though Blackett's attraction to Communism caused some disputation. It's odd to think that Bernard Lovell was then no more than a promising young lecturer in Blackett's department.

Michael was again a close friend of Hicks and Jewkes, the economists. It is an example of his prescience in all things that he became extremely interested – about 1946 – in the problems of money supply. They actually had an extraordinary machine which illustrated most dramatically the circulation of money in the economy, with the effects of the inputs on the outputs – a primitive version of the modern Treasury computer. Of course, the trigger to Michael's interest – I often saw him putting the machine through its paces – was his passion for freedom, an enjoyment of which is not totally divorced from matters of money supply.

Quite apart from the side of him you are going to consider this weekend, Michael was an absolute charmer, a shining light in Manchester society. Some of you might think that that is not to say much. But in my view, and I have lived long in London, Manchester society produced a mixture of all the talents found by me nowhere else. There in the same room you would find physicists and editors, heads of industry and neuro-surgeons. In this brilliantly mingled company, Michael was an admired figure. He was so courteous and so gentle – 'sweet' was the word that sprang to many lips to describe 'Mischie' –

a name for him his friends like to use, though Magda felt no one outside the family had the right to call him so.

Yet he was clearly a man of strength. When a matter touching principle was raised, he would be taken over by a deep seriousness, and there was a power in him at such times. His whole life lived up to the thought we shall be discussing this weekend.

There seemed no limits to his knowledge, far beyond the bounds of science and philosophy, and talking to him enlivened the mind and often carried you to a peak of excitement. Yet I remember his smile and the twinkling eyes. He was a very good friend to have.

INTRODUCTION

Thomas F. Torrance

The various contributions that make up this book have their origin in a conference held in November 1978 at St. Catherine's, Cumberland Lodge, Windsor, with the theme, 'Belief in Science and in Christian Life: the relevance of Michael Polanyi's thought for Christian Faith and Life'. A two-fold intention lay behind it: to reconsider certain Christian convictions in the context of the on-going scientific revolution of our times, and to make constructive use of the help we believe we can derive from the works of Michael Polanyi, one of the greatest scientist-philosophers of our age. The six addresses given at the conference were planned and prepared with a view to eventual publication and in the hope that they would combine to make a coherent book which might be of help to other people, and for some might even open the gates of faith. Rewriting has been undertaken for this purpose and in the light of the encouraging discussion to which the addresses gave rise. This is not meant to be a technical work either in theology or in the philosophy of science, but is designed for a wider public not trained in theology or science who seek a deeper understanding of the Christian faith and want to grasp something of its inner reasonableness. They need rational support for their beliefs, but instinctively they know that it must come from the very foundations on which those beliefs rest.

We live today in a time of great disturbance, for a vast shift in the thinking of mankind is taking place in which deeply entrenched patterns in our culture are breaking up and new patterns are struggling to be born. Evidently there is always a period in the course of such a transition from one settled outlook to another when wild fluctuations in belief and thought are apt to arise, and there is considerable confusion in people's minds. Such is the state of affairs we now find almost everywhere — indeed the upheaval may well be greater than at any time since the early centuries of the Christian era — but all this is surely the prelude to a more deeply settled, unitary outlook in which Christian and scientific understanding of the created universe will draw closer together.

A profound change of this kind has been taking place in natural science since the beginning of this century. Many of our long-accepted ideas have proved inadequate, and even the classical formulations of natural law have been found to break down again and again before the astonishing revelations of nature. In our scientific investigation into the structures of the universe, from the tiniest particles to the greatest clusters of stars, we find more and more a dynamic orderliness which defies our attempts to account for it in the old way, by breaking everything down into physical and chemical elements and then connecting them externally together according to rigid rules of cause and effect until the whole universe is made out to be a vast mechanistic system. The more our modern instruments have enabled us to penetrate into the deep internal connections in nature, not least in the sub-atomic realm, the more we find disclosed a spontaneous and dynamic kind of order arising out of mutation and adjustment which undergirds and interpenetrates what previously we had regarded as random and disorderly events, so that the notion of the universe as the product merely of blind chance and necessity has been seriously undermined. The kind of order we find in the universe in field after field of our inquiries is richer, subtler and more variable than we had realised or computed from within the narrow limits of our stereotyped thought-forms. Really to grasp nature in its natural order we have to develop more appropriate ways of understanding and interpretation of an *integrative* kind, rather like the basic acts of perception, recognition and apprehension with which we are familiar in our everyday experience as rational persons, in which knowing and being and acting are inextricably woven together. This newer and deeper way of discovering the secrets of nature, as Einstein used to insist, is only an extension and refinement of our ordinary experience and knowledge.

Few people have grasped the significance of this revolution in our scientific approach to knowledge as profoundly as Michael Polanyi, who took part in it and drew out its implications with unrivalled sensitivity, delicacy and balance. He was a physician and a chemist who shared to the full the claim of modern science that all our knowledge must be grounded upon experience. The real world is so different from what we expect and so full of surprises that we must allow it to reveal itself to us. That is what experimental science is about: experiments are questions that we put to nature for nature itself to answer. Then in the light of what nature tells us in this way we revise and deepen our knowledge of it. Regarded in this way science is the continued penetration into the nature of things enabling us to grasp them in their inner structure and reality.

Unfortunately, however, as Polanyi tells us, modern science manifests certain inner contradictions and obsessions which are destructive of its own aims, for its concentration on abstract and formalistic thought cuts off the reason from the very base in experience on which it operates. At the same time it operates with a dualism between mind and matter, which leads it to concentrate upon matter, to the exclusion of mind, as though knowledge were restricted to visible, tangible facts and their interconnections, and as though there could be knowledge even of material realities apart from the personal activity of a knower. On this view, it seems, science could only give an absurd account of itself in which the mind was missing! The emphasis upon an impersonal, detached approach is 'meant to exclude from scientific knowledge all subjective bias and prejudice, so that it can be truly 'objective' — but it is forgotten that only a person is capable of self-criticism and of distinguishing what he knows from his subjective states, and therefore of appreciating the bearing of human thought upon experience, and so it is only a person who can engage truly in objective and scientific operations. According to Polanyi, any scientific research pursued in a detached, impersonal, materialist way isolates itself from man's higher faculties and thereby restricts its range and power of discernment and understanding. What science needs is a new approach in which it overcomes the damaging split between subject and object, mind and matter, or thought and experience, and recovers the natural unity of knowing and being, for without the integrative way of thinking that such a rational balance brings, science can only obstruct its own attempts to grasp the finer and more delicate patterns embedded in nature. That is why he devoted so much effort to restoring the role of 'personal knowledge' in scientific activity in which the personal and the objective are fused together.

Behind all this, of course, lie recent advances in fundamental science of the greatest importance, particularly after the great switch in thought initiated by Planck and Einstein with quantum theory and relativity theory. They have gone far to establishing science upon a deeper basis in reality, and to restoring in it the integrity of man's personal and rational inquiry into the meaning of the universe. Here old analytical methods have given way to synthesising ways of thought which are more capable of grasping the many levels of existence and integrating them in such a way that a gradient of meaning rises through them all in which the higher intangible levels of reality are found to be possessed of the deepest significance, so that man's natural knowledge expands continuously into the knowledge of the supernatural. It is to this unifying outlook that Michael Polanyi has contributed so creatively in restoring the balance of our cognitive powers and in reconciling science to man by restoring science to its true purpose.

It was evidently not Polanyi's main intention, in reconstructing the scientific basis of man's knowledge of the universe, to make room for religious faith or knowledge of God, but he was nevertheless aware of doing just that, as a by-product of his argumentation. Not only has he helped to release Christian faith from pressure by the conception of the universe as a closed mechanistic system of cause and effect, but he has shown us that in the most rigorous scientific activity the human mind cannot operate outside a framework of beliefs which, though formally unprovable, play an essential role in guiding the thrust of inquiry into the hidden meaning of things. That is to say, he showed that scientific activity, and indeed all rational activity, operate with an inner relation between faith and reason similar to that found in Christian theology in its movement of inquiry from faith to understanding, so that his declared intention in rehabilitating the role of belief in scientific activity was also aimed at the foundation of religious faith. Further, Polanyi showed that the freedom and integrity of science cannot be sustained except through a dedicated submission to transcendent or spiritual reality over which we have no control: and that cannot be done on secular grounds alone. Thus he held, on the one hand, that rigorous pursuit of pure science, which requires a framework of responsible commitment to the claims of reality, brings to light ultimate obligations which direct us to God, but he held also, on the other hand, that the freedom of science and the community which supports it cannot be maintained without the spiritual foundations and ultimate beliefs mediated to human society through the tradition of the Christian Church.

This position adopted by Michael Polanyi reflects the far-reaching change that has come about in the relations of science and theology. Properly pursued they cannot be opposed to one another but are rather to be regarded as complementing one another in our understanding of the meaning of the created universe in which God has planted us, and within which he makes himself known to us. This does not imply that belief in God and knowledge of him are built upon the foundations of natural science, for they have their own proper ground in the self-revelation of God, but since that takes place within this world of space and time into which natural science inquires, we are obliged to bring our belief and knowledge of God to expression in the patterns of thought and speech which we gain under the impact of God's creation upon us. Theology and science arise and take shape within the one world which God has made and upon which he has conferred the rational order that makes it accessible to our scientific inquiries. Hence constant dialogue with natural science enabling us to share in its remarkable discoveries of God's handiwork can only be helpful to us in developing our knowledge of God, even when we allow our minds, as we surely must, to be lifted above the world of nature that they may acquire patterns of belief and thought really appropriate to God under the transforming impact of his self-communication to us in Jesus Christ.

That is what we try to do in the different chapters of this book, as again and again we quarry from the thought of Michael Polanyi. It is not our intention in what follows specifically to expound his thought, at least in any detail, but to learn from him as a scientist how on our own ground we may rethink certain aspects of the Christian faith and bring them to rational expression in such a way as to intensify their continuing relevance for us in the universe God has created.

I

THE FRAMEWORK OF BELIEF

Thomas F. Torrance

It is a long established and generally accepted habit to think of faith in a two-fold contrast between faith and sight and between faith and reason. This is a way of thinking that stems, in part at least, from the Biblical roots of Judaism and Christianity, but the contrasting positions have often been pushed to extreme points where their original signifi-' cance has been badly distorted. That is what happened, for example, during the Enlightenment, or the so-called 'Age of Reason', which has left its mark upon popular understanding, as is everywhere evident today, in scientific as well as in non-scientific circles. It is in scientific thought, however, that a more balanced view of faith or belief has steadily built up and is now exerting its impact beyond the frontiers of natural science, restoring to the foundations of human knowledge an integration which it had lost.

The contrast between *faith and sight* is rather sharpened, as different people have pointed out, when one compares the Judaeo-Christian habit of mind with that of the Hellenic tradition. Thus Martin Buber argued that 'the Greeks established the hegemony of the sense of sight over the other senses, thus making the optical world into *the* world, into which the data of the other senses are now to be entered'.[1] Similarly John Macmurray used to show that the Greek form of consciousness, evident in Hellenic science and art, rested upon aesthetic insight.[2] In the Hebraic habit of mind, hearing and seeing, word and vision, were not disjoined, but the stress is upon word and hearing as shaping the basic mode of understanding and giving primacy to faith over sight. This had to do with the conviction that the invisible and eternal God is the overwhelming reality with whom we have to do. Since he constitutes the creative ground of man's being and knowing, it is through trust and reliance on him that human existence is to be ordered in the world. Along with this conviction went another that, whereas knowledge by sight depends on the see-er who must rely on himself, obedient hearing of the Word of God gives rise to knowledge in which man does not rely on himself but on God. Hence even when an Old Testament prophet speaks of 'seeing a vision' of God, it is made clear that the vision is governed by the Word of God mediated through it, over which the prophet has no control. It is through the response of faith to that Word, and in reliance upon God who makes himself known in this way, that man is established in his understanding, and all his visible and tangible existence is thereby given true form and direction.

It is in continuity with this tradition that the New Testament statements about belief or faith are to be understood. We recall how frequently in his teaching Jesus called for belief in his message and in the Word of God it embodied, and how he persistently emphasised the primacy of believing over seeing. 'Because you have seen me,' said the resurrected Jesus to St. Thomas, 'you have believed; blessed are they who have not seen and yet have believed.'[3] That was consistent with his refusal to give the crowds any compelling perceptible demonstration of his divine Sonship, for he confronted them on the ground of his own self-evidencing truth alone. This is not to say that the miraculous 'signs' which Jesus offered had nothing to do with making him known, but that their purpose was to point people away to God who is to be known only through believing obedience, and to confront them with the power of the truth which alone can make them free.

Much the same teaching was given by St. Paul. Belief refers to a hidden reality, something which is not visibly or tangibly present but is accessible to us through the medium of word. Thus God is believed not on the strength of anything else but of his own self-revelation, and as through his Word he commands our knowledge on the ground of his own self-evidencing spiritual reality. The faith that arises in us through the Word is a kind of hearing in which we respond to the faithfulness of God himself[4], and in which we are so obediently and irreversibly committed to God, that faith becomes a habit of mind and a way of life. 'We walk by faith and not by sight.'[5] Because the divine reality with which we are in contact through faith transcends our experience in space and time, the scope of faith is directed not only beyond what is visible to the invisible, but beyond what is temporal to the eternal: thus faith in God merges into hope and anticipates the ultimate vision of God.[6]

This biblical contrast between faith and sight does not imply a contrast between faith and knowledge or therefore between faith and reason, for faith rests upon the ultimate reality of God himself who is more truly knowable than any other reality and who, though he cannot be demonstrated from any other ground inferior to himself, constitutes the ground on which all truly rational knowledge reposes. There is, then, a contrast between two different kinds of demonstration and two different kinds of apprehension, which St. Paul distinguishes in terms of divine and worldly widsom.[7] God is discerned in his own transcendent reality and truth in a spiritual way in accordance with his divine nature as Spirit, i.e. by a demonstration of the Spirit and power of God himself; and not in a carnal way through the self-willed operation of a human mind alienated from its proper ground in God, i.e. not by a demonstration based on the arbitrary subjective processes of the reason turned in upon itself. Faith, as St. Paul spoke of it, is the opposite of a merely subjective state of affairs. It is precisely because in faith we are grasped by the ultimate reality of God that in faith we are freed from emprisonment in the darkness of our own preconceptions, fantasies and errors. That is the reason for the unshakeable confidence of faith, for it is caught up in the unswerving faithfulness and reliability of the truth and love of God which have laid hold upon us in Jesus Christ and is steadfastly undergirded by them. Faith reposes not on the weakness of the believer but on the power and constancy of its divine object.

In patristic times the Christian view of the relation faith and sight and faith and reason was often held to be summarised by The Epistle to the Hebrews: 'Faith is the substance (*hypostasis*) of things hoped for, the evidence (*elegchos*) of things not seen. . . . By faith we understand that the worlds have been framed by the word of God, so that what is seen has not been made out of things which do appear'.[8] Faith has its own support beyond itself on which it relies, its own evidential or rational grounds, in virtue of which it has its own way of penetrating beyond appearances to the objective orderly structure controlling them, that is, to their creative source in the Word of God. This was the understanding of faith that was so richly developed, for example, by Clement of Alexandria in the second century. Faith, he held, is the placing of our mind on that which is, but that is exactly what we mean by basic scientific knowledge (*episteme*), which (if we take the Greek expression literally) is the standing of our mind on objective

3

realities.[9] That is to say, faith describes the connection between hu[man]
thought and reality which rational or scientific knowledge [pre-]
supposes and on which it must rely in any further inquiry. He[nce]
Clement was very fond of citing from the Old Testament, 'If you [will]
not believe, neither will you understand'.[10]

There are two kinds of demonstration. The first is that in wh[ich]
we allow our understanding to fall under the compelling self-evide[nce]
of reality. That is not only the most basic kind of proof that there [can]
be, but the only one we can have in respect of an unseen or hith[erto]
unknown reality. Without that kind of demonstration and the c[on-]
ceptual assent to reality it calls forth from us, knowledge would n[ot]
get off the ground, and all that would happen would be a retreat [in]to
our false preconceptions. The second kind of demonstration is tha[t of]
the logical connection of ideas, such as we make use of in geometr[ic]
reasoning, where we are not concerned with making someth[ing]
appear in its own truth but with clarifying the knowledge we h[ave]
already gained of it. Demonstrative reasoning of this kind help[s to]
give consistency to our beliefs. What leads people to disbelieve, h[ow-]
ever, is always preconceived opinion, for it obstructs them f[rom]
apprehending realities in accordance with their own natures and[on]
their own evidential grounds. It is the task of scientific inquiry,
not least in theological matters, Clement claimed, to distinguish [the]
true from the false by deploying the conceptual assent or judg[ment]
embedded in faith in such a way as to allow what we are investiga[ting]
to be grasped more faithfully in accordance with what it really [is in]
its own nature. Hence in our inquiry into divine revelation faith [and]
theology must be concerned from beginning to end to respect [the]
nature of God as he discloses himself to us and to learn how to th[ink]
and speak of him appropriately and worthily. Because of the t[ran-]
scendent holiness and purity of God, a disciplined contemplation [of]
him is required of the believing mind so that its power of spiri[tual]
discernment may be steadily refined in a movement not only f[rom]
faith to deeper faith but from faith to vision.[11]

St. Augustine, whom we may take as our example of wes[tern]
patristic thought, was also fond of citing the same passage from Isa[iah,]
'If you will not believe, you will not understand'.[12] Again and ag[ain]
he emphasised that we must not seek to understand that we may [be-]
lieve, but must believe that we may understand.[13] There is a d[eep]
reciprocal relation between faith and reason, for 'everyone who [be-]
lieves thinks, but thinks in believing and believes in thinking',[14]

4

St. Augustine tends to connect faith with prior assent yielded to truth on the basis of authority, which gives access to understanding and is a necessary stage in reasonable inquiry.[15] Understanding contributes to the comprehension of what is believed and thus reinforces faith by establishing it on the intrinsic authority of the truth itself and not merely on an external teaching authority. Faith is understanding's step and understanding is faith's reward. The movement from faith to understanding involves a progressive informing of the mind in the course of which the eyes of faith are strengthened and its vision is purified. 'Faith has its own eyes with which it somehow sees to be true what it does not yet see, and with which it sees most surely that it does not yet see what it believes.'[16] However, according to St. Augustine, a distinction must be drawn between the rational cognition of temporal things which he calls 'knowledge', and the intellectual cognition of eternal things which he calls 'wisdom'. In the light of that distinction it must be said that faith, even though it pertains to eternal things, is itself a temporal thing and must pass away, although it is necessary if through our earthly pilgrimage we are eventually to attain to eternal things when the knowledge of faith will give place to wisdom.[17]

The teaching of Clement and Augustine can be taken as fairly representative of the balanced view of faith in its relation to our perceptive and cognitive powers that prevailed in classical Christian thought and affected Western culture for many centuries. However, it was not without serious problems, for beneath the thought of Clement and Augustine alike there lay a deep cleavage in the relation between what they called the 'sensible' and the 'intelligible' worlds, which threatened to disrupt not only the wholeness of the Judaeo-Christian outlook on the created universe but the balanced view of faith and knowledge. Platonic and especially Neoplatonic influence in both East and West gave rise to a dangerous dualism in faith and knowledge in which intelligibility and spirituality both took on a radically otherworldly orientation in accordance with which not only nature but man's involvement in physical existence was given little more than symbolical interpretation. This was nowhere more evident than in the pressure toward a symbolical understanding of the Christian sacraments which became the centre of long controversy. In order to restore the balance high mediaeval thought resorted to the Aristotelian principle that there is nothing in the mind which is not first in the senses, and systematically integrated rational knowledge through ideas abstracted from sense experience and elaborated within a framework of strictly causal connections. The dualist tendencies in the Augustinian tradition were restrained, but there remained a cleavage between supernatural and natural knowledge, still apparent (at least in traditional Roman Catholic treatises) in a split between the doctrine of the Triune God based on divine revelation and the doctrine of the One God based on natural knowledge.

It was doubtless because the classical understanding of the relation between faith and knowledge was being undermined that Western mediaeval thought devoted so much energy to reconciling faith and reason. It certainly achieved a new synthesis, but in a very different way from that which we find in the thought of Clement of Alexandria, for its acceptance of the idea that the only really evident knowledge is that which we are given through the senses, meant that it had to work with a notion of faith that is not evidentially ground on objective reality, or its intrinsic intelligibility except in some mediated way. Faith tended to be defined as assent to the truth given on the ground of authority, whereas reason assents to the truth on the ground of its own self-evidence. This gap between faith and rational knowledge appeared at its widest in the teaching of William of Ockham, who found himself having to bridge the gap through appealing to the power of God to cause intuitive knowledge of non-evident realities, and indeed, he claimed, of non-existent objects.[18] That is how theology comes by the 'creditive ideas' with which it operates.[19] Basically, however, the teaching of St. Thomas was not so very different, but for him the gap between the human intellect and the reality of God was bridged in a more Augustinian way through an infusion of divine grace and light. Here faith is regarded as the act of the intellect assenting to divine truth under the command of a will moved by God's grace, and not on the ground of its immediate self-evidence.[20] The human mind is disposed by divine grace to accept what the Church proposes for belief, and in that process it is endowed with an *additional* 'light of faith which makes it see the things that are believed', so that although the intellect does not have the 'certainty of evidence' it nevertheless is made to rest, not on propositions of belief, but through faith on the saving reality of God himself.[21]

Since the general framework of connections, with which the prevailing Augustinian-Aristotelian outlook operated, was built up under the overarching dominance of the concept of final cause, it gave rise to a view of nature as impregnated with divine causes and to the development of a human culture, including natural science, as oriented

6

toward God. However, as soon as its inherent dualism led to the segregation of material and efficient causes as the proper subject for scientific investigation (i.e. the restriction of natural science to the questions what and how), the phenomenalist emphasis upon sense experience turned the basic orientation of thought in the opposite direction, not toward God but toward the sensible or material world. This was reinforced by an even severer dualism embedded in the quantifying and mechanical approach of Galileo and given massive systematic formalisation by Newton. Thus there arose not only the mechanistic conception of the universe but a narrow-minded materialist and positivist conception of knowledge which rigidly excluded any realm of intelligibility beyond the evidence of the senses, denigrating it as 'metaphysical' or 'mystical'. This concentration upon phenomena or appearances, upon observable and tangible magnitudes which are quantifiable, gave rise to what Michael Polanyi called the 'massive modern absurdity', the limitation of rational knowledge entirely to what can be tested by reference to observations or logically deduced from them.[22]

It was inevitable that the scholastic way of relating faith and knowledge through infused grace and external authority, which was revived after the Reformation (not least in England through Richard Hooker), should come under severe strain and begin to fall apart as soon as sensory evidence alone was held to be admissible for rational knowledge and the new empirical scientific approach called in question all preconceived ideas or beliefs imposed by external authority. It was early in this development that John Locke produced the paradigm 'contradistinction between faith and reason' in which many generations of people have been trapped. Since the human mind, he held, begins with a clean slate, all its knowledge comes from experience, by sensation or reflection, and is built up step by step through demonstration operating with 'visible certain connections'. Rational knowledge is thus equated with demonstrable knowledge and is sharply contrasted with belief which is no more than an 'ungrounded persuasion' of the mind, for it is only extraneously and not evidently related to the thing believed.[23] This had the effect of rejecting the rational acceptability of any claim to knowledge resting upon some internal light of faith or assurance or some external authority such as 'traditional revelation'. That is to say, faith was not respected as a source of knowledge beyond the range of observation and demonstrative reasoning for it is only a private persuasion or opinion.[24] 'For whatever is not capable of demonstration . . . is not, unless it be self-evident, capable to produce knowledge, how well grounded and great soever the assurance of faith may be wherewith it is received; but faith it is still, and not knowledge; persuasion, and not certainty. This is the highest the nature of the thing will permit us to go in matters of revealed religion, which are therefore called matters of faith; a persuasion of our own minds, short of knowledge, is the last result that determines us in such truths.'[25]

It was not only in the sphere of 'revealed religion' that this antithesis between faith and knowledge had a deleterious effect, for, as Michael Polanyi argued, in disrupting the balance of man's cognitive powers it damaged the very foundations of knowledge, and laid the basis for the modern rationalism and scientism which have so cruelly shackled the human spirit. 'Belief is here', Polanyi wrote (with reference to the passage from Locke just cited), 'no longer a higher power that reveals to us knowledge lying beyond the range of observation and reason, but a mere personal acceptance which falls far short of empirical and rational demonstrability. The mutual position of the two Augustinian levels is inverted . . . Here lies the break by which the critical mind repudiated one of its two cognitive faculties and tried completely to rely on the remainder. Belief was so thoroughly discredited that, apart from specially privileged opportunities, such as may still be granted to the holding and profession of religious beliefs, modern man lost his capacity to accept any explicit statement as his own belief. All belief was reduced to the status of subjectivity: to that of an imperfection by which knowledge fell short of university.'[26]

That is the problematic state of affairs which we inherited at the beginning of the twentieth century and which is still to be found in popular science and general thought, but in fundamental science the situation began to change very radically especially with the early work of Einstein and his steady rejection of the positivist stance in knowledge. Along with the basic change in the whole structure of physical science which Einstein traced back to James Clerk Maxwell, there had to go a rejection of the abstractive procedures whereby patterns of thought are torn away from the objective intelligible ground in reality on which they rest. Hence Einstein set about getting rid of the gap that had been posited in modern thought between mathematical knowledge and empirical knowledge, for all our knowing at whatever level involves an inseparable intertwining of theoretical and empirical elements. While all knowledge of reality starts with

8

experience and ends with it, there is no logical way to that knowledge through deduction from observations, for there is no logical bridge between our ideas and experience. We have to employ what Einstein called an 'intuitive' mode of apprehension, resting on a sympathetic understanding of nature, to penetrate into the intelligible features inherent in nature, if we are to grasp the elementary principles and formulate the physical laws which apply in nature.[27] Einstein was equally insistent in attacking any kind of *a priori* approach to knowledge which was another way of tearing apart the forms of our thought from their ontological ground in reality, and could not escape being trapped in subjectivism.[28] Thus he inverted the whole way of thinking that derived from Locke and restored a non-logical relation between the mind and reality to the foundations of knowledge and at the same time restored a way of thinking which is not tied exclusively to visible connections but which penetrates beneath or behind appearances to an invisible relatedness inherent in nature which controls appearances.[29] 'God does not wear his heart on his sleeve', as Einstein used to say.[30] But that means that all Einstein's thought operated within the framework of controlling belief in the intelligibility and reliability of nature which belonged to the very core of what Einstein understood by religious experience.[31]

It was this Einsteinian restoration of scientific knowledge to its ontological foundations in objective reality that appealed to Michael Polanyi, for it accorded with his own basic insight and findings as a physical scientist.[32] He insisted that we must recognise belief or intuitive apprehension once more as the source of knowledge from which our acts of discovery take their rise, for it is in belief that we are in direct touch with reality, in belief that our minds are open to the invisible realm of intelligibility independent of ourselves, and through belief that we entrust our minds to the orderly and reliable nature of the universe. Behind and permeating all our scientific activity, reaching from end to end of our analyses and investigations, there is an elemental, unshakeable faith in the rational nature of things, but faith also in the possibility of grasping the real world with our concepts, and faith in the truth over which we have no control but in the service of which our human rationality stands or falls. Faith and rationality are intrinsically interlocked with one another. No human intelligence, Polanyi claimed, however critical or original, can operate outside such a context of faith, for it is within that context that there arises within us, under compulsion from the reality of the world

9

we experience, an operative set of convictions or a framework of beliefs which prompts and guides our inquiries and controls our interpretation of data.[33] They are the ultimate beliefs or normative insights on which we rely as premises in any authentic thrust toward truth and which finally give the arguments we advance their real force, even if they have to be revised in the process. Far from suppressing these beliefs, therefore, we ought rather to bring them out into the open, clarify them, and put them to the test in the actual processes of scientific investigation and in any leap forward of scientific discovery and verification.[34]

It must be granted, of course, that these basic beliefs or convictions are not themselves directly or logically demonstrable, for they have to be assumed in any attempt at rational proof or disproof. They have what Einstein called an 'extra-logical' status although they are nonetheless rational, for they do not have to do with the relations of ideas to ideas, but with the relations of ideas to being which cannot be put into logical form. They are logically prior to any demonstration for they have to do with the bearing of the reason on the nature and structure of things, which all explicit forms of reasoning are intended to serve and without which they are blind and impotent. Since this is the case, it would be irrational to contrast faith and reason, for faith is the very mode of rationality adopted by the reason in its fidelity to what it seeks to understand. We believe in order that we may understand, as the Fathers of the Church used to insist, and in the course of deepening our understanding we clarify and test our beliefs and thereby strengthen their hold upon our minds.[35]

Here, then, we find ourselves back at the roots of the Judaeo-Christian understanding of faith in its relation to sight and reason. But does this faith imply some special form of understanding, some additional insight divinely infused into us which we may have apart from evidential grounds of knowledge, such as was held so widely in mediaeval times? The answer must surely be that faith 'sees' not with any special faculty of vision on the part of the observer, but with the powers of the reality seen. That is another way of saying that faith is correlated with the intrinsic rationality of the object and its self-evidencing reality and revealing power, which applies in different measure to the functioning of perception and the functioning of faith. While in both we are committed to the recognition of reality independent of ourselves, in perception we rely more on ourselves as observers, but in faith we rely more on the nature of the reality beyond ourselves. Understandably, therefore, faith in God calls for a mode of response in accordance with his nature as the transcendent ground of all created being and intelligibility, but for that very reason faith involves a rational and not a blind commitment to God, in the course of which there ought to take place a steady sifting out of true from false belief.

In showing that all knowledge rests upon faith and develops under the guidance of a framework of belief Michael Polanyi has much to offer us in elucidating the nature and functioning of faith in the understanding and life of the Church today. In what follows, therefore, we shall single our certain aspects of Polanyi's teaching and draw out their implications for our purpose.

Belief is objectively, not subjectively, grounded

All our personal and rational activity operates with two poles, a subjective pole and an objective pole. The subjective pole is the knowing, believing, acting person, and the objective pole is 'the other', either another person or some reality independent of himself. A person acts rationally when he interacts with the other and does not confuse it with himself, i.e. when he looks away from himself to the other. Polanyi constantly illustrates this by referring to the use of a stick to explore a cavern or the way a blind man feels his way by tapping with a stick.[36] He is only vaguely aware of the stick in his hand, for all his concentration is directed to the objects he contacts through his stick beyond himself. That is how all meaning arises, when we look away *from* ourselves *to* something else. That *from/to* relation is the semantic aspect of knowing in which we meaningfully make contact with some reality external to or independent of ourselves and attend to what it signifies from itself.[37] Thus, for example, in reading a book we do not focus our attention on the letters and sentences themselves merely as marks on paper, nor do we treat them as some way of giving expression to ourselves, but we attend to that to which they *refer* beyond, for it is in that objective reference that their significance lies. It is within this *from/to* or objective relationship, according to Polanyi, that belief arises, as a kind of listening obedience of the mind to reality, without which the human reason cannot begin to operate.[38] 'Thought can live only on grounds which we adopt in the service of a reality to which we submit.'[39] 'Truth is something that can be thought of only by believing it.'[40]

Proper belief, therefore, cannot be said to be irrational or blind, for it is a cognitive assent to some aspect of reality, a basic act of recognition in which our minds respond to a pattern or structure inherent in the world around us which imprints itself upon them. It is through such a basic act of assent, for example, that geometric patterns arise in our minds when we perceive crystalline formations in the rocks: we do not impose those patterns upon the rocks; the rocks impose them on our minds, and we respond by an act of acknowledgment. It is indeed upon such basic acts of acknowledgment or recognition by way of concepts and statements that all our scientific knowledge is built up. On the other hand, it must be said that it is not any pattern in nature that has this effect on us, some kind of meaningless collocation of marks or a jumble of sounds that is a mere noise: it must be a coherent pattern or an orderly structure of some kind, to which we react by way of acknowledgment and assent.[41] Our fundamental beliefs are just such basic acts of acknowledgment in response to some intelligibility inherent in the nature of things, that is, to some meaningful order or message-laden pattern; but as such they pivot upon the *objective pole* of the knowing relationship, and cannot be reduced to a merely subjective state of our consciousness. Beliefs are certainly personal acts, as we shall see, for it is only persons who are capable of engaging in objective operations, in which they refer meaningfully away from themselves and distinguish orderly patterns and structures as having reality independent of their perceptions. Belief has to do with the elemental interaction between persons and realities other than themselves, entailing a recognition of their independent reality and truth.[42]

I have been describing the nature and status of belief in scientific knowledge, but all this applies fully to the nature and status of belief in our knowledge of God. Here too our basic convictions and beliefs are unprovable – for example, that God is love and is the creative source of all order in the universe – but they arise within us as basic acts of assent and acknowledgment on the part of our minds to divine Reality which we cannot know except on grounds of service and obedient listening or submission. There are, of course, significant differences between religious beliefs and scientific beliefs, but the differences have to do, not with their status as beliefs, so much as with the nature of that in which we believe and in the kind of intelligibility inherent in what we believe. Thus where the objective pole of the *from/to* relation is a person, the mode of assent and the nature of the conviction aroused is appropriately personal and not impersonal, i.e. in the form of trust. And where the kind of intelligibility inherent in the objective pole is to be characterised in terms of 'word' rather than 'number' (appropriate for determinate, quantifiable realities), the kind of acknowledgment requried is word-orientated, where 'listening obedience' is preculiarly appropriate as the New Testament makes clear in its account of faith as evoked and sustained by the address of God's Word. Moreover, where the objective pole is some other creaturely reality, an impersonal object or a personal being, our relationship with it is on the same creaturely level (although as observers or knowers we may well occupy a logical level above it)', but where the objective pole is God the Creator our relationship to him can only be one of reverence in which we look up, and not across or down, to him, so that faith in actual contact with the reality of God appropriately assumes the form of worshipping acknowledgment and adoration.[43] Within these important differences, however, religious belief remains essentially the same as scientific belief in that it is the direct bearing of the mind upon reality in a basic act of cognitive assent or acknowledgment, and as such is the ground of knowledge.

Belief is a basic conviction that arises in our minds compulsorily but not necessarily

Belief is not something that is freely chosen or arbitrary, that is, without evidential grounds, for that would be highly subjective, a mere fancy. Nor is it something hypothetical or conditional, for then it would not be genuine, since we would entertain it, as it were, with our fingers crossed. Rather does belief arise in us, as we have seen, because it is thrust upon us by the nature of the reality with which we are in experiential contact. It arises as we allow our minds to fall under the compelling power of an intelligible structure or order inherent in the nature of things which we cannot rationally or in good conscience resist. That is to say, belief has to be understood strictly within the context of rational submission to the claims of reality upon us and of obligation towards the truth laid upon us by truth itself. It is this external anchoring of belief that saves it from being subjective or arbitrary, for it binds belief to what is independently and universally true. Properly speaking, therefore, a belief can be held only with (what Polanyi calls) 'universal intent', i.e. within the framework of a commitment to reality in which we assent to the universal validity of what we believe.[44] Belief and truth are thus correlated with one another. Regarded in this way, truth is the external pole of belief, and belief, far from being merely a subjective or private concern, is the obedience of the mind to objective reality in recognition of its universal and normative authority. Hence to destroy belief, Polanyi argues, would be to deny all truth.[45]

Belief would be destroyed, however, if there were posited a merely necessary relation between belief and reality, that is, if beliefs were causally imposed on our minds by the external world, for that would eliminate freedom to believe or not to believe as we judge we must and so relieve us of personal responsibility for our beliefs.[46] Of course, if beliefs were causally imposed on us that would also eliminate the possibility of error, for we would not be put in a position where we are thrown back upon ourselves as rational centres capable of deliberate activity and conscious judgment in the face of alternate possibilities, and where we find ourselves under obligation to respond to the claims of reality upon us in right and appropriate ways.[47] Thus while belief pivots upon the objective pole of the knowing relation, the subjective pole must be given its proper if subordinate place, i.e. the role of the person or rational agent in believing, and believing as he feels he ought to believe in fidelity to the truth. As Polanyi expresses it: 'The freedom of the subjective person to do as he pleases is overruled by the freedom of the responsible person to act as he must'.[48] This is what is so distinctive about scientific belief, the combination of personal and compulsive elements in it. These two elements Polanyi brings together in his notion of *commitment* in which freedom and obligation, conscience and obedience, are bound inseparably together under the overarching authority of truth.[49]

There are two other important aspects of scientific belief which we must note at this point: the *exclusiveness* and the *open range* of belief.

Since belief arises within a context of commitment to reality which we recognise to be universally binding, it entails a judgment which excludes a divergent belief.[50] When we adopt one way of looking at things, Polanyi points out, we destroy at the same time some alternate way of seeing them. Thus, as we have noted, the observation of words and sentences as mere marks on paper destroys their significance as meaningful signs which have to be read as referring to something else. Or again, we may think of the mutually exclusive approaches to the same situation in terms of causes and reasons: one seeks to understand some aspect of nature in terms of external causal connections, and another seeks to understand it by penetrating into its inner reasons or intelligibility.[51] It is because there are alternate ways of looking at things that we put them against one another, so that we

14

can examine the case for some theory and the case against it, but when the theory achieves the status of a natural law, it is formulated in such a way that other possibilities are thereby excluded. Thus out of alternate constructions that may be placed upon a set of data, one will be universally acknowledged and the others rejected. Under the compelling claims of reality we affirm this to be true and that to be false, and we affirm our belief with universal intent: we can do no other because of its normative character. That is what Polanyi called 'the logic of endorsement' or 'affirmation' which lies at the very heart of science.[52]

On the other hand, since belief arises in our minds under the pressure of reality and its inherent intelligibility, it remains open toward whatever may yet be revealed from the side of reality. But since reality has a capacity for disclosing itself in yet unthought of ways in the future, belief which bears upon that reality is locked into a range of intelligibility that reaches far beyond, so that by its very nature belief is stretched out toward the truth which it has only partially grasped and can have only a provisional form until the final outcome.[53] It is belief with an open range in its focus. This implies that the affirmation of a belief cannot be fully justified at the moment it is being held since it is oriented toward a future fulfilment, but it also means that belief contains a heuristic impulse evoked through correlation to a reality possessed of a significance that transcends our experience or apprehension at any moment. In other words, belief, as Polanyi understands it, is tied up with the fact that we know more than we can tell, that our basic affirmations indicate more than we can specify. That is the kind of belief that lies behind the thrust of scientific inquiry and discovery, but since that is the kind of belief we bring to our affirmation of natural laws (the 'dogmas of science', as Whitehead called them), they are constantly open to revision in the light of the reality in which we believe.

Once again it is rather startling to find that when Polanyi analyses the structure of scientific belief like this, he comes up with an account that might well have followed the pattern of Christian belief. He was clearly aware of this comparison, as he shows in the cross-references he makes from time to time to the nature and function of Christian faith, but they are evidently made by way of reflections subsequent to his analysis. At any rate, it is manifest that the logic of scientific belief is basically the same in scientific knowledge and in theological knowledge. If it is true in natural science, it is certainly true in Christianity

15

that belief arises in us compulsorily yet freely under the constraint of the creative reality and self-revelation of God in Jesus Christ. 'Every belief is both a free gift and the payment of a tribute exacted from us. It is given on the personal responsibility of the believer, yet in the clear assumption that he cannot do otherwise.'[54] That is precisely how St. Paul understood Christian faith, but the words I have cited from Polanyi describe scientific belief. Because the grace of God comes to us unconditionally but brings with it unconditional obligations, faith that is grounded on grace carries with it a deep sense of both freedom and compulsion. We believe freely but believe as we must. Faith is a free responsible act of our own but it is anchored beyond itself in the faithfulness of God which undergirds and sustains it so that it acquires by the grace of God a strength beyond anything we can give it. Therefore in faith it is not on our own believing that we rely but on him in whom we believe, upon the grasp of God's love which will not let us go. Epistemologically expressed: the objective pole of Christian belief is truth, truth over which we have no control, but truth that apprehends us and makes us free.

• Further, like scientific belief, Christian belief is also a cognitive act which we cannot in good conscience avoid when face to face with the self-disclosing reality of God in Jesus Christ, but unlike scientific belief, as we have already noticed, the mode of rationality this involves is 'word' and not 'number'. In natural science knowing begins with basic acts of assent by way of acknowledgment of a rationality inherent in physical nature and operates correspondingly with 'recognition-concepts' or 'recognition-statements' upon which the subsequent structure of scientific knowledge is grounded. In theology, however, knowing takes its rise with basic acts of assent by way of acknowledgment of the Word inherent in God which is addressed to us in the mode of its human incarnation in Jesus Christ, so that theological knowing operates with 'recognition-concepts' or 'recognition-statements' of a different kind, which (following a late Mediaeval theologian, John Major) we may call 'intuitive auditions' or 'auditive intuitions', upon which the kerygmatic or dogmatic structure of all Christian knowledge rests.

Here also, however, we find the same fundamental characteristics noted by Polanyi, the exclusiveness and the open range of belief. Faith in the one God rules out the possibility of our having other gods. Faith in Jesus Christ as 'the Way, the Truth and the Life' excudes access to the Father by any other way than Christ. Christian faith within the framework of commitment to the incarnation of the Son of God who as incarnate is of one being with the Father, when formulated in terms of its intrinsic rationality, operates like a natural law in science which excludes the entertainment of other possibilities or disqualifies any other theoretic construction of the same data. This is why the Nicene-Constantinopolitan Creed expressing convictions which the Church found to be universally compelling, and which has subsequently become the universally acknowledged Creed of all Christendom, by its intrinsic structure excludes alternative doctrine as arbitrary innovation in the face of God's self-revelation in Jesus Christ, i.e. as heretical deviation from the truth. On the other hand, while the Nicene-Constantinopolitan Creed expresses what we are obliged to acknowledge within the general framework of the Church's commitment to the reality of God's self-revelation in Jesus Christ, it is all prefaced by *Credo, I believe*. That is to say, everything that is asserted here falls within the compass of belief pivoting upon the objective reality of God which, far more than than the reality of nature or of the universe, is characterised by an inexaustible range of yet undisclosed truth. Correlated to the open range of belief which indicates more than can be expressed, the formal statements of the Creed are incomplete and inadequate, but are as such revisable in the light of the unlimited intelligibility of God to which they direct us. Because Christian faith by its very nature as faith in God has an open, eschatological scope, by asserting our doctrinal convictions under the rubric of *belief* we claim that they fall short of their intention and are inadequate in themselves. Hence we say with St. Paul that we do not claim that we have already apprehended or have already arrived at the end, but we press on in order to apprehend that for which we have already been apprehended by Christ Jesus.[55]

The formation and function of beliefs within a developing framework of belief and tradition

We believe in order that we may understand and as we progress in understanding something our basic beliefs are tested and clarified in the light of it. In the course of this deepening interrelation between belief and understanding we develop a set of normative beliefs which functions as an interpretative framework for the critical and constructive work of further inquiry. Such is 'the fiduciary programme', Polanyi claims, with which scientific knowledge operates, that is, a self-expanding system of belief in which initial beliefs and subsequent beliefs mutually relate to one another. While our fundamental beliefs are continuously reconsidered in the course of such a process, that takes place only within the scope of their own basic premises in a movement which is admittedly circular.[56] In elucidation of this circularity a two-fold distinction may be drawn between implicit and explicit beliefs, and between ultimate and working beliefs.

Pascal once pointed out with reference to mathematical proof that it is impossible to operate only with explicit definitions, for in defining anything in one set of terms we presuppose another set of terms, but to define them we would presuppose still other terms, and so on in an endless process. Similarly Polanyi points out that we cannot reach a formal definition by cutting it off from the informal, undefined base on which it rests, for that would make nonsense of it. Thus in any explicit definition we rely upon implicit, undefined knowledge of something else, but this implicit knowledge becomes more fully known as we rely on it in making an explicit definition.[57] That, as he understands it, is the relation between implicit and explicit belief: explicit beliefs are justified by relying on implicit beliefs which direct and control their use in on-going scientific inquiry, and implicit beliefs are clarified in that process. Indeed they are strengthened in their hold upon us in so far as the system of expanding belief which they underly and integrate successfully functions as an interpretative frame of thought coping with a wider range of data and as a heuristic instrument opening up new, unanticipated areas of knowledge.[58]

At this point it should be noted that although our implicit and explicit beliefs bear on one another in this circular way within the one fiduciary framework, we are not trapped in the vicious circle of our own subjectivity, for genuine belief, whether implicit or explicit, is linked to an objective pole in the reality to which it refers and in relation to which it stands or falls.[59] A self-interpretative and self-expanding system of belief operates and holds good only within the context of such a commitment to a reality independent of belief and only in so far as it is anchored in the intelligibility inherent in that reality. Our explicit beliefs are held to be justified through their integration with our implicit beliefs, but since our implicit beliefs cannot be justified from any other ground than that on which they claim to rest, the whole system of belief stands or falls with its power to command our acceptance. Is the acceptance of the system as a whole consistent with the submission to reality which the scientific reason face to face with its compelling rationality must yield in a relation of ultimate obligation? In normal scientific activity such an acceptance is not in question precisely because our normative beliefs are implicit, but from time to time open conflicts in the area of our explicit beliefs arise when our implicit beliefs which integrate the whole system are brought to the surface: and we are confronted with the decision to accept or reject the system as a whole.[60] This is the kind of decision with which we are faced today in the mutually exclusive outlooks of the new science with its rejection of determinism and of positivist or empiricist science with its deterministic rejection of belief in any scientific system. Behind all this lies the question of ultimate beliefs and their relation to working beliefs, to which we now turn.

In spite of the disclaimers of the positivists we all operate with ultimate beliefs – 'to claim that you strictly refrain from believing anything that could be disproved is merely to cloak your own will to believe your beliefs behind a false pretence of self-critical severity'.[61] In so far as our beliefs are ultimate or fundamental, Polanyi argues, they are 'irrefutable as well as unprovable'.[62] There is no higher or wider system with reference to which they may be demonstrated. Ultimate beliefs give rise to a framework of thought of which they are the constituent determinants. They stake the ground they constitute as the only ground for their justification, and thereby deny disproof any ground on which it might take its stand. A signal example of such an ultimate belief is the conviction that there is order in the universe, which we would have to assume in order to prove; but without such a conviction we could not believe that the universe is accessible to scientific inquiry. It is under the controlling power of ultimate beliefs such as this that we develop our working beliefs, such as the unique status of light, with reference to which we seek to understand and explain the structure of the space-time universe. Now any belief, implicit or explicit, not least any ultimate belief, if it is conceivable is conceivably false, and is therefore open to questioning and testing. Since we can offer no independent demonstration of ultimate beliefs to which we are nevertheless committed, we must test our commitments through responsible self-criticism, in order to distinguish genuinely ultimate beliefs from any subjective notions or imaginations on our part, for we can accept as ultimate only what is objectively forced on us by the intrinsic intelligibility, truth and authority of the reality in the field of our inquiry, which it would be intellectual suicide for us to deny.[63]

Thus our ulitmate beliefs arise under the pressure of elemental aspects of reality seeking realisation, as it were, in our minds, and as such become determining constituents of our whole frame of belief and affect the entire shape and scope of our thought. They provide the normative insights which promote and prime our inquiries; they exercise a critical and directive function in the way we put our questions, interpret our experiences, and weigh evidence. It is under the power of their bearing on all this that we form our judgments and make our decisions and carry through the reasoning operations of our inquiries to their true ends. It is the extent to which we allow these ultimate beliefs in which we share to have this role in our arguments and theories that they have their really persuasive power.

Ultimate beliefs are general beliefs which we cannot reasonably avoid, for they repose upon the unalterable nature of things, but other particular beliefs call for acceptance within the expanding system of belief and its general commitment to reality, operative or working beliefs, as we may call them. They are beliefs which contain explicit affirmations which we come to hold by rejecting alternatives which, it may be claimed, can be reasonably held. As such these working beliefs coincide with explicit beliefs or assertions of science such as we formulate in natural laws and which, once formulated, also exercise a regulative control on our on-going scientific inquiry. The very possibility of alternatives in these regulative beliefs or natural laws with which we operate in science, is itself grounded in the ultimate belief in the contingency of the universe, i.e. that the universe might have been otherwise, that it could well have been different. It is belief in the contingency of the universe that is also the determining ground for the conviction that in our search for order and regularity in the universe we cannot do without experimental questioning of nature itself, and that our understanding of the order and regularity of the universe which we formulate in natural laws and theories may well have to be changed. Thus once again we come up against the inexhaustible novelty of reality upon which Polanyi laid such stress. 'To hold a natural law to be true is to believe that its presence may reveal itself in yet unknown and perhaps unthinkable consequences; it is to believe that natural laws are features of a reality which as such will continue to bear consequences inexhaustibly.'[64]

On the other hand, the explicit formulation of working beliefs and their affirmations provides our basic beliefs with an articulate framework which can considerably extend the range and thrust of the heuristic impulse deriving from our ultimate beliefs. Thus startling scientific discoveries have been made possible through the creation of a machinery of precise thought such as rigorous symbolical and formal systems which have opened up new paths to intuition. That was already evident in the invention of language and writing which equipped man's informal powers with a cultural machinery, enormously increasing the range of human comprehension. The new symbolic languages of science are only an extension of that achievement, but like language and writing they have to be regarded as conceptual instruments forged in the service of our ultimate, implicit beliefs in their thrust through an ever-expanding system of belief to an ever deeper apprehension of the universe.[65]

We have seen that all true belief has both an objective and a subjective pole. This applies, however, also to the framework or system of belief with which science operates, for while that framework is correlated objectively to the structures of reality, it is also embodied in a community which embodies it in its social structure and imparts to it the force of its ontological reference. In the first instance the framework of belief is embodied in the existence and continuity of a scientific community, that is in groups of like-minded scientific inquirers or in the world-wide community of scientists who share a common belief in the existence of reality and its intelligibility, and who exercise among themselves control through mutual criticism and conjoint verification of their work, in the course of which their common beliefs are tested and clarified and deepened. It is only within the continuity of such a supporting community and the tradition it carries that the basic beliefs are transmitted from generation to generation in such a way as to give power and thrust to its search for deeper and deeper understanding. But all the time the community's normative beliefs are, or ought to be, steadily re-examined in the course of this expansion in understanding, so that they are continuously put to the test and reappropriated. This can be done, however, only through consistent, responsible commitment to the intelligibility of reality which is the one source of true belief and the ground of its universal authority and validity.[66] In the second instance, this expanding framework of belief is embodied in human society which supports the scientific community and its programme of research, for it is within that human and social structure that all our basic beliefs in their bearing upon the real world around us are generated. While those beliefs arise in implicit and tacit ways, and with no more than the spontaneous self-correcting devices each community builds up in its will for survival, without them even in their uncritical form our scientific investigations would not even get off the ground. A great deal depends therefore on the maintenance within the society of an open relation with the structures of the real world which allows for the spontaneous emergence of basic beliefs of this kind, but also upon the disciplined tradition of the social and scientific community within which science is pursued and the standards which it sets for itself.[67] It was for this reason that Polanyi devoted so much of his attention to the promotion of a free society dedicated to a distinctive set of beliefs in common commitment to the truth over which we have no control but in engagement with which we are liberated from obstructive prejudices and self-destructive tendencies, in authoritarianism and scepticism alike, with which humanity has so often been afflicted.[68]

Polanyi's account of the embodiment and functioning of a self-expanding system of belief in the structure and tradition of the community supporting the scientific enterprise is based on a deeper insight into the nature of knowledge and its communication than that offered by scientific rationalism deploying only explicit statements based on tangible data and derived from them by formal inferences. Admittedly this has an important bearing upon the Christian doctrine of the Church and the formation and communication of normative beliefs within its developing tradition, in accordance with which over many centuries its dogmatic convictions are formulated, but not without considerable critical testing through the mutual faith and combined authority of the membership of the Church in its on-going commitment to the reality of God's self-revelation in Jesus Christ. We must leave that aside here, but in order to conclude our discussion we may recall how Polanyi reinforced his insight into the role of belief in the development of knowledge by analysing the actual process of learning in which each of us has shared from childhood, for that would seem to offer us points of immediate relevance for our theme.

It will be sufficient for us to consider three overlapping stages in the child's intellectual growth.

1. The emergence of an inarticulate framework of belief and understanding.[69] By the time we are four or five years of age, each of us has learned a staggering amount of physics, merely through constant interaction with our environment, the animate and the inanimate, the personal and the impersonal world around us. Through processes of mutual adjustment and adaption our consciousness becomes structured in accordance with the coherences, patterns and order

inherent in the nature of things, in which ultimate beliefs and working beliefs are built into the fabric of our intellectual development in such a way that we can never go back on them – although the whole process of learning, correction, and revision of course goes on.[70] Here we have already in operation a matrix of implicit belief grounded on reality upon which the child relies in assimilating new experiences and forming explicit beliefs in terms of which he adapts his understanding to the intelligibilities of the world around him and increases his hold on reality. This is what Polanyi calls the *tacit dimension*,[71] a state of affairs built into the rational structure of personal being in which a child knows more than he can tell, so that learning takes the form of a process of discovery in reliance upon the heuristic acts of assent to the nature of reality embedded in his implicit ultimate beliefs.

2. The development of articulate frameworks of belief and understanding.[72] This takes place right away with the acquisition of speech which is absorbed uncritically from the community and tradition into which we are born. But as we are born into a language, we are also born into a set of beliefs about the nature of things – and here we are concerned mainly with the rise of explicit beliefs.[73] These beliefs are transmitted through the tradition of convictions in which we participate, but they reach us along with our acquisition of conceptual instruments such as linguistic and numerical systems which serve to enhance the child's inarticulate mental powers. Polanyi remarks with astonishment on the deployment of the infant mind.[74] When we stop to think of it, in learning that two times two equals four, the child is thinking conjunctively on three levels at the same time, the word level, the number or symbolical level, and the empirical level, and has no difficulty in doing so – yet that turns out to be precisely the structure of the most developed science. However, while the child acquires these systems of explicit belief and conviction, along with articulate frameworks, he cannot learn from the explicit instruction of others how to operate the rules of conceptual or symbolic symbols. That can be learned only through example and apprenticeship, only through participating with others in the way they rely on the tacit dimension of belief and insight in manipulating articulate frameworks of belief and concept.[75] Hence Polanyi finds that considerably more emphasis must be paid to community learning within an on-going tradition of belief and understanding, in which he makes use of the notions of participation and indwelling.[76]

3. The development of independent judgment and critical

thought.[77] Our basic beliefs, implicit and explicit, are acquired un-critically in the course of our early development and education or subsequent apprenticeship to scientists, but no subsequent critical ex-amination of these basic beliefs, Polanyi argues, can ever eliminate the 'fiducial' elements in our thinking. If that were possible, it would mean the eradication of all creative power in our thinking and the stultification of scientific discovery. The development of critical power is no less necessary, but at this point it is all-important that the child or young person should retain a proper balance in his cognitive powers between criticism and belief, for it is upon that balance that his deployment of analytical and integrative modes of thought de-pends.[78] That is why, as we have seen, Polanyi was determined to restore the balance of our cognitive powers by restoring to the heart of science the full place and function of belief, for without it we lose the basic passion for discovery and the thrust of creative science.

The elucidation that Michael Polanyi has offered us of the forma-tion and function of normative beliefs, alike in the developing struc-ture of scientific knowledge and in our individual intellectual develop-ment from earliest childhood, throws not a little light on the historical development of Christian theology as it is embodied in the life and mission of the Church and the emergence of our own beliefs within the on-going tradition of the Church's worship and teaching. Let me refer only to three elements in this where Polanyi's account reinforces the Church's interpretation of its own developing framework of belief and tradition.

First, the deep interlocking of faith, worship and understanding under the guidance of the ultimate beliefs imprinted upon the mind of the Church in its commitment to God's self-revelation in Jesus Christ. This takes place both in the Christian home where the basic beliefs of the child are generated and nurtured and in the continuing fellow-ship of the Church at the ground level of doxological and evangelical experience deriving from regular meditation upon the Word of God and regular participation in liturgical worship. That is the context of faith and understanding within which there arises what Polanyi calls 'heuristic vision'[79] that primes our prayerful search for God and opens our minds for new insights into divine truth.

Second, the development of intuition and judgment which shape the formulation of our explicit beliefs within the framework of the compelling claims of Christ upon us and of our commitment to him. That takes place as under the guidance of the rule of faith, or the interpretative framework of belief, handed down to us from the irreversible apostolic foundation of the Church in Christ, but also within the expansion of our understanding as through Christ and in the Spirit we are given ever new access into the truth of God as he is in himself. Here we have a movement of thought which corresponds rather startlingly with that which Polanyi describes in natural science, namely, the process of continued penetration into the intelligible nature of things which, while gaining increasing width and depth, takes place within the scope of the premises of our ultimate beliefs.

Third, the interrelation between implicit and explicit belief, informal and formal acts of knowledge, helps us to appreciate genuine theological operations. On the one hand, theological formalisation is seen as the equipping of our tacit beliefs with precise machinery that enhances their power; and on the other hand, theological operations are found to outrun the Church's formalisations at any specific time and to anticipate new and more adequate modes of thought. Yet all that relies finally upon the profound spirituality both embodied in the Church's tradition and transcending it, a spirituality that is locked through ultimate beliefs into the inner intelligible relations in God himself, as Father, Son and Holy Spirit. Trinitarian worship and Trinitarian theology thus provide constant restructuring of the life and understanding of the Church in the image of God.

NOTES TO CHAPTER I

1. Martin Buber, *The Eclipse of God*, 1952, p. 40.
2. John Macmurray, *The Clue to History*, 1938, p. 22f.
3. St. John 20.29.
4. Galatians 3.2; Romans 1.5; 16.25.
5. 2 Corinthians 5.7.
6. 1 Corinthians 13.12f; 2 Corinthians 4.18.
7. 1 Corinthians 2.5ff.
8. Hebrews 11.1, 3.
9. Clement of Alexandria, *Stromateis* IV.xxii, 143.2-3. For further references see, T. F. Torrance, in *Oikonomia. Heilsgeschichte als Thema der Theologie* (ed. by F. Christ, 1966), p. 224.
10. Isaiah 7.9.
11. Clement, *Stromateis* VIII.iii-viii; cf. *Oikonomia*, p. 225ff.
12. Augustine, *De libero arbitrio*, 1.4; 11.2; *Sermones* XVIII.3; XLIII.3; *Epistolae* CXX.1, 3, etc.
13. Augustine, *In Joannis Evangelium* XXVII.9; XXIX.6; XL.9; *De Trinitate*, VII.5; *Epistolae* CXX.1, 3, etc.

14. Augustine, *De praedestinatione sanctorum* 11.5.
15. Augustine, *De ordine* II.ix, 26f; *De vera religione* XXIV.45.
16. Augustine, *Epistolae* CXX.2.8.
17. Augustine, *De Trinitate* XII.2.2.f; 3.3f; 13.21; 14.22f; 15.25; XIII.1.2f; XIV.1.3.
18. Ockham, *Quodlibeta septem* I.13-14; 5.5; 6.6.
19. Ockham, *Quodlibeta septem* 5.5; 6.6; *In librum secundum sententiarum* 15.E.
20. Thomas Aquinas, *Summa theologiae* II.11.q.2, a.9.
21. Thomas Aquinas, *Summa theologiae* II.11.q.1, a.4, ad 3; q.1, a.5, ad 1; *Scriptum super sententiis* III, d.2, a.1, ad 4; *Summa theologiae* II.11, q.1, a.2, ad 2; q.5, a.3; *In Boethii de Trinitate* 1.q.1, ad 2, ad 6 and ad 7. A better construction could be put on St. Thomas' thought if he is taken to mean that faith sees not by an interior vision of its own but by the light of the object seen.
22. M. Polanyi, *Personal Knowledge*, 1958, p. 9.
23. John Locke, *Essay concerning Human Understanding*, 1690, IV.xv.1-3; xix, 11f.
24. John Locke, *op. cit.*, IV.xvi.14; xviii.2-11; xix.1-15; cf. xx.1ff.
25. John Locke, *A Third Letter for Toleration*, 1692, vol. 5, 12th edit. 1801, p. 144.
26. Michael Polanyi, *Personal Knowledge*, p. 266.
27. A. Einstein, *The World as I See It*, 1935, pp. 125f, 133, 135f; P. A. Schilpp, *Albert Einstein: Philosopher-Scientist*, 1951, pp. 11f, 81, 273ff, 362ff, 373f, 401, 406f.
28. A. Einstein, *The World as I See It*, p. 174; *Out of My Later Years*, 1950, p. 61; P. A. Schilpp, *op. cit.*, pp. 674-80.
29. See especially the account of Einstein's conception of science offered by F. S. C. Northrop, P. A. Schilpp, *op. cit.*, pp. 387-407, with which Einstein expressed agreement, p. 683.
30. Cf. F. S. C. Northrop, *Man, Nature and God*, 1962, p. 209f.
31. A. Einstein, *Out of My Later Years*, pp. 30, 60f; *The World as I See It*, p. 131; P. A. Schilpp, *op. cit.*, p. 3f.
32. M. Polanyi, 'From Copernicus to Einstein', *Encounter*, Sept. 1955, pp. 54-63; *Personal Knowledge*, ch. 1, on 'Objectivity', pp. 3-17. For the historical and conceptual background to this, see Richard Gelwick, *The Way of Discovery*, 1977, pp. 24ff, 29ff.
33. M. Polanyi, *Personal Knowledge*, pp. 264-68.
34. *Science, Faith and Society*, new edition with new preface, 1964, pp. 7-19, 85-90.
35. F. Schwarz (editor), *Scientific Thought and Social Reality: Essays by Michael Polanyi*, 1974, pp. 67-81; 116-30.
36. *Personal Knowledge*, pp. 63ff, 211ff; *The Tacit Dimension*, 1967, pp. 25, 76ff, 87 etc.
37. *The Tacit Dimension*, pp. 11ff; *Knowing and Being*, 1969, pp. 140f, 161, 182, 218.
38. *The Logic of Liberty*, 1951, p. 21; *Personal Knowledge*, pp. 57, 116; *Knowing and Being*, pp. 145, 153f, 161f, 182ff, 193ff.
39. *The Tacit Dimension*, xi.
40. *Personal Knowledge*, p. 305.
41. *Personal Knowledge*, pp. 33-48.
42. *The Tacit Dimension*, pp. 25, 76f, 87.
43. *The Study of Man*, 1959, pp. 93-99. Polanyi points out that 'We need reverence to perceive greatness, even as we need a telescope to observe the spiral nebulae.' p. 96.
44. *Personal Knowledge*, pp. 65, 302f, 308f, 311f; *Knowing and Being*, pp. 33, 132ff.
45. *Personal Knowledge*, p. 286; cf. 305.

46. *Personal Knowledge*, pp. 64ff, 269, 303, 308ff, 320ff; *Science, Faith and Society*, pp. 42ff, 63ff.
47. *The Study of Man*, pp. 54ff, 74ff.
48. *Personal Knowledge*, p. 309.
49. *Personal Knowledge*, ch. 10 on 'Commitment', pp. 299-324.
50. *Scientific Thought and Social Reality*, pp. 58-66.
51. *The Logic of Liberty*, pp. 20ff, 25.
52. *Personal Knowledge*, ch. 8 on 'The Logic of Affirmation', especially pp. 253-61.
53. *Tacit Dimension*, pp. 23f, 32f, 68f, 87; *Knowing and Being*, pp. 82, 119f, 133, 138, 168.
54. *Scientific Thought and Social Reality*, p. 79.
55. Philippians, 3.12f.
56. M. Polanyi, *Personal Knowledge*, pp. 264ff.
57. *Science, Faith and Society*, pp. 10ff, 43ff, 85ff; *Personal Knowledge*, pp. 160ff, 264ff, 286ff, 299ff.
58. *Personal Knowledge*, pp. 286-94; cf. *Knowing and Being*, pp. 105ff, 124ff, 138ff.
59. *Personal Knowledge*, pp. 289f, 292f, 299f.
60. *Personal Knowledge*, pp. 150ff, 195ff.
61. *Personal Knowledge*, p. 271.
62. *Ibid.*
63. *Personal Knowledge*, pp. 299ff.
64. *Knowing and Being*, p. 138.
65. See the long chapter on 'Articulation' in *Personal Knowledge*, pp. 69-131.
66. *Personal Knowledge*, pp. 203-45 on 'Conviviality'. *The Tacit Dimension*, pp. 55-92 on 'A Society of Explorers'.
67. See also T. F. Torrance, 'The Open Universe and the Free Society', *Ethics in Science and Medicine*, vol. 6.3, Nov. 1979, pp. 145-53.
68. See *The Logic of Liberty, Science, Faith and Society, Scientific Thought and Social Reality*, and also the earlier work *The Contempt of Freedom*, 1940. Cf. Richard Gelwick, *op. cit.*, pp. 35ff, 42ff, 111ff.
69. *Personal Knowledge*, pp. 69ff.
70. *Personal Knowledge*, pp. 75f, 333; *Knowing and Being*, pp. 212f.
71. *Personal Knowledge*, pp. 86ff, 95ff, 213ff, etc.; *The Tacit Dimension, passim; Knowing and Being*, pp. 133, 138ff, 160ff.
72. *Personal Knowledge*, pp. 82ff.
73. *Personal Knowledge*, pp. 74f, 101ff, 112f; *Scientific Thought and Social Reality*, pp. 61ff, 75ff.
74. *The Tacit Dimension*, p. 61.
75. *Personal Knowledge*, pp. 49f, 53f, 173f, 195f, 207ff, 374ff; *Science, Faith and Society*, pp. 42ff, 52f, 63ff.
76. *Knowing and Being*, pp. 105ff, 134f, 148f, 151f, 160f; *The Tacit Dimension*, 17f, 30, 61, etc.
77. *Personal Knowledge*, pp. 53ff; *Science, Faith and Society*, pp. 43f; *The Tacit Dimension*, pp. 61f, 68f.
78. *Personal Knowledge*, pp. 171, 264f, 272ff, 292ff, 312ff; cf. *Knowing and Being*, pp. 194f, 212f.
79. *Personal Knowledge*, p. 199, 280ff.

2

INDWELLING: FORMAL AND NON-FORMAL ELEMENTS IN FAITH AND LIFE

JOHN C. PUDDEFOOT

Introduction: The Crisis of Credibility

Christians have been told so often and for so long by so many people, both inside the Church and outside it, that what they believe is irrational, impossible or simply absurd, that now they almost believe it themselves. Much of this criticism has come from people who profess doubts about the adequacy of the biblical evidence for much of the belief supposedly based upon it. Lacking any conviction themselves about God as revealed in Jesus Christ – we might say 'lacking any Christian experience' – they apply themselves to the task of demonstrating, on the basis of formal, textual inadequacy, that the experiences and convictions of others must thus be erroneous.

I doubt that anyone convinced of the validity of their Christian convictions would pretend to be able to express with complete adequacy the nature of those convictions. Nevertheless, the persuasive passions evoked by a living relationship with God demand of us that we at least attempt such expression. In what follows I shall call all conscious or unconscious communications 'formal' expressions, and the experiences and knowledge they fail adequately to describe 'non-formal', parts of which at least are in fact unformalisable.

In seeking to re-establish a coherent conceptual framework for Christian faith and life we shall use Polanyi's concept of *dual control* coupled with his insistence upon *indwelling* the particulars of an object of interest as *subsidiaries* in order, by a process he calls *tacit integration*, to derive a true perception of their *focal* meaning. I hope to show that the essentially non-formal individual and collective knowledge achieved by the Church provides a true and reliable ground for our interpretation of formal texts.

Because, for reasons which will become clear, I am convinced that the Bible is not an 'axiom system' for Christianity, but rather a companion and guide formalised by the Hebrews and the Early Church in response to man's perception of the ineffable truth of God, I propose to seek validation for my arguments by appealing, not to the results logically derivable from the biblical witness, but to the *focal* meaning to be perceived by indwelling the biblical record as *subsidiary*. Thus I do not assert things solely because the Bible does, but because I am passionately persuaded that they are true, and because my indwelling of the biblical formalisation of the understanding of the Hebrews and the Early Church corroborates my view.

This paper is an attempt to articulate my own non-formal perception of a conceptual ground the significance of which I can but vaguely see. It follows that despite the inevitable inadequacy of such formalisation, if those who read it will commit themselves to the attempt to understand the programme I have outlined, we may together achieve an appreciation of this ground which is richer than I could achieve myself.

Language

Polanyi, as you may recall, rejects as inadequate the associationist theory of language.[2] Instead he claims that the child, in learning a language, or the adult in learning a second language, accepts from the community to which the language 'belongs' the meanings indicated by that language, and makes them his own. The drive to communicate leads both to receive such linguistic frameworks 'into' themselves and to indwell those frameworks as subsidiaries whereby to achieve their focal intention, which is to communicate real meaning.

The appropriation of language by an individual is the linguistic equivalent of the intellectual appropriation of reality in science as a given to which we are obliged to respond with integrity. The 'language' constitutes such a given reality, the meaning of which we accredit and thus reaffirm in our appropriation of it. The community which sets its own standards in, say, science or art, is thus a special case of a nation which sets its own standards by accrediting a language as mutually acceptable and meaningful. The individual learning the language thus participates in a conviviality which as a whole sets the multi-personal standards by which the objective criteria of meaning and truth are determined. Polanyi repeatedly insists that to buy sceptical consistency by refusing to accredit such meaning can only be at the cost of imbecility.

By locating the authority of the Bible and Christian doctrine in the shared accrediting of the Christian community as a conviviality, far from losing their status, they find their true places as some of the necessary 'given realities' of the Christian Church and its distinctive language about God.

Just as one cannot question an entire language in that language, so in Christianity it is nonsensical to attempt to adopt a stance from which to decide 'objectively' what of the Bible and past doctrine can remain *unless* that stance be one defined by the being of the Church as a higher authority, an authority based solely upon its continual indwelling in study, worship and prayer of the presence of the living God. Biblical criticism, therefore, consists not so much in 'editing' the Bible or 'remaking' Christian doctrine as in re-establishing, by indwelling the formalisations of past community understanding, an appropriate framework of current non-formal perception in which the Bible and past doctrine can resonate in the way a tuning-fork is amplified when place over an appropriate volume of air.

It is to this programme, the re-establishment of true non-formal grounds for the Christian faith and life that I have devoted the main body of this paper.

Mathematics

I would like to begin by considering why it is that we are sometimes unable to understand formal expressions. To do so I would like, if I may, to describe my own failure to become a mathematician.

I once rejoiced under the illusion that I *was* a mathematician. I say 'illusion' because what I really was was a manipulator of mathematical formulae. After going to university to read mathematics, I soon found that whilst I could follow – I deliberately avoid saying 'understand' – proofs of theorems in text-books, I was often unable to adapt those proofs to problems related to them.

We have all done mathematics at some time. First one learns the basic symbolism, then follows the logical sequence of steps through to the QED. Nothing could be simpler. Yet some people are unable to follow even these processess. Equivalently, some of us are so confused by French vocabulary and grammar that we never progress to real French literature. My problem – and I was not alone – was that whilst able to 'follow' the mechanics of the proof, in turning to related problems I found that I lacked the *conceptual apparatus* necessary to adapt the theorem to the new circumstance. Looking back, I now realise that whilst following the symbolic operations I had paid such close attention to the letter that I had lost the overall meaning of the letters. In Polanyi's terms, the subsidiaries had become focal. The true mathematician reads such symbols in the same way Polanyi's 'accomplished linguist' reads a letter; he assimilates its meaning by indwelling the words, but afterwords is left only with the meaning, having forgotten which language it was written in.

We can thus see that whilst following the mechanics is *necessary* if we are to indwell and attain the focal meaning, it is not *sufficient*.

I could also never understand why my tutors were so unwilling to teach me the mystical method whereby to solve problems. It was only some years later that I realised that they were not unwilling, but unable. Since the integrative processes whereby we attain to focal comprehension of the symbols is essentially unformalisable, as Polanyi repeatedly demonstrates, how could my tutors describe it to me? All they could do was to teach by example, leaving the pupil as apprentice to make the necessary integrations whereby to obtain their *skill*.

We can see that the processes whereby we understand the writings or formalisations of others depend upon the same tacit skills whereby we control and assess articulations of our own non-formal perceptions.

Nevertheless, for the student the crucial question is 'Why am I unable to perform these tacit integrations with the facility shown by others?' The answer is because the conceptual world reflected in the formal expressions is *not part of his experience*. The mathematicians who first discovered the theorems we now study did not start with a set of axioms or formulae and simply manipulate them until something 'came up'. They started from what they perceived to be a problem from comparison of different fields of study, or from paradoxes arising from previous results. From such observations (obtained by indwelling the various fields) plus, of course, a degree of manipulative ability, they extracted certain common properties as a formalised set. This set they then attempted to describe in the most economical way – they attempted to axiomatise it. But having axiomatised the system, new hypotheses are not derived by trial and error. Instead, hypotheses arising from the original intuitive grounds of the system may be proved by showing that they are derivable from the previously accredited axiom set. They then become *theorems*. Thus mathematicians, by a process of indwelling, extraction/abstraction and simplification/ axiomatisation provide the world with a tool whereby to test new hypotheses. Belief in the universal validity of these results comes from the accrediting of their colleagues, and the richness of the implications of their results as they 'resonate' in other minds.

Most mathematicians fail because they lack the heuristic framework which gave rise to the systems they study. Unable to dwell in the birthgrounds of the axiomatised systems they are forced to attempt problem-solving by manipulation of formulae, aided by what little insight into the background of the formulae they can derive. Thus, instead of starting (as the great creative mathematician does) from a conviction that a certain hypothesis is true (a conviction derived from commitment to, and indwelling of its real basis) they begin from the 'given-ness' of the axiom system. Admittedly, trial and error come into proof sometimes, but hypotheses are seldom if ever derived in this way.

In this long digression into the non-formal conceptual basis of mathematics I have attempted to demonstrate how formal systems, unless controlled by a heuristic vision derived from commitment to the truth of a reality *independent* of that formalisation and the enquirer, can only lead us into incoherent manipulation of symbols. Reluctant to believe that the fault lies in ourselves, the next step is often to deny the adequacy or reliability of those formalisations. How often do students go to their teachers complaining 'the question's wrong!' As a corollary we can see how misleading is the view that mathematics is an impersonal, indeed depersonalised discipline. Great mathematical discoveries come from the passionate searching of committed individuals, and mathematical truths from the collective accrediting of those results by the mathematical community.

Theology and Belief

As a brief illustration of the consequences of this analysis, let us consider the question of whether or not one need be a believer in order to be a theologian.

If I tried to write mathematics without understanding what I was doing I might succeed in deceiving the uninitiated with my symbols, but a competent mathematician would not be fooled for very long. I could only succeed in fooling him if I confined myself to copying results derived by other people, perhaps altering the surface features a little. As soon as I attempt new work my lack of an overall perception of the meaning reflected in my symbols will become apparent.

Of course, the question 'need one *understand* God in order to write theology' is impertinent, but the question 'need one *believe*, and thus be passionately committed to the attempt to understand God in order to write theology?' is legitimate, and forms a closer parallel with the mathematical case. Polanyi was influenced by the great patristic and mediaeval slogans: *nisi credideritis non intelligetis*; *credo ut intelligam*; *fides quaerens intellectum* ('Unless you believe you will not understand'; 'I believe in order to understand'; 'faith seeking understanding'.) Yet so much theology places the integrity of man's so-called 'rationality' at the head of its priorities (it is concerned not to abandon man's objectivity, dispassionateness, fairness) that it allows its concern to preserve that integrity to destroy the very message which calls the legitimacy of that integrity most into question. The Christian Gospel is of the man who called our self-appointed values into question and demanded of us that we be reborn in body, mind and spirit, a demand that incorporates the rebirth of the way we think and act, the way we live and move and have our being. Christ demands faith of man, the faith to dwell in him.

The grounds of mathematical abstraction are the realities with which the mathematician is concerned; the Bible is *itself* a formalisation of a perception of the reality with which it is concerned. The biblical accounts must thus, rather than being reduced to sufficient factors, first be integrated to their focal meaning. The 'theorems' derived by such abstractive criticism, when applied to the texts themselves, thus cannot but produce fragmentation for they have been derived without the personal and communal interpretative effort within which the texts can come alive and resonate. If one adds up all the criticisms which have been levelled against the Birth narratives, the Incarnation, the Resurrection, the miracles, the eschatological sayings, the parables, and the dependence of Jesus' words upon the wisdom literature and contemporary Jewish teaching, not to forget to delete all the 'Son of Man', 'Son of God', 'Messiah' and 'Christ' sayings as attributions of the post-Resurrection Church, then it is clear that not much remains. The reductionist biblical critic has made himself redundant and demonstrated his own folly by proving that the texts with which he has concerned himself are unworthy of the effort. He has made the same mistake as the failed mathematician. Unable to perceive the non-formal interpretative ground of the text, he has subordinated it to the text, and claimed that since the text is defective the

33

non-formal perception is impossible. This is like denying the possibility of Shakespeare's plays because monkeys cannot produce them from typewriters. The authority of the text comes solely from the continuous accrediting of it by the community of interpretation, the Church. Thus the biblical witness, whilst a *necessary* ingredient in the Christian gospel – it is hard to imagine where we would be without it – is not, and must not be allowed to become, *sufficient*. The Bible and Christian doctrine are the rails whereby we measure our continuity with the past, but the non-formal interpretative framework of the community of faith in accrediting them as such cannot be set aside; that is the mistake of so much biblical criticism.

Dual Control

So far we have emphasised the process whereby the non-formal perceptions and intentions of an individual or community control its formalisations and its interpretation of the formalisations of others. The Bible and Christian doctrine are thus controlled by the self-set standards of the community of the Church in its perception of the living reality of God. But just as the Church constrains the range of interpretation allowed, so the Bible and the doctrines of the past lay constraints upon the range of the Church. This general process of mutual, but asymmetrical constraint Polanyi calls *dual control*. After a brief summary of this process we shall show how the community uses self-examination to limit erroneous interpretations of past formalisations, and then proceed to the question of the individual Church member both as disciple and pioneer.

The kinds of organisms which can exist are limited by the properties of matter as described by physics and chemistry, and those organisms which do exist are dependent upon physical and chemical processes for their health. Without physics and chemistry there could be no life, but live organisms exercise control over physics and chemistry in a way not itself reducible to physics and chemistry. Physics and chemistry are necessary, but not sufficient to account for the existence of life. Similarly, without language man's powers of articulation and his superiority over other animals would be severely curtailed, but the uses to which he puts that language are not themselves attributable to language. Language enables man to record and store information, and facilitates economic handling of ideas, but the drives and intentions which govern such recording and enquiring are not reducible to the languages used. Language too, then, is necessary for much of man's life, but not sufficient to explain it. The lower principles, physics and chemistry or language, may limit my action to prevent me flying or articulating certain skills or convictions, but they do not in themselves decide where I walk or how I express myself. In both examples there is a hierarchical principle involved which is unformalisable, and renders the whole irreducible to its necessary parts.

Polanyi writes:

'This may resolve the paradox that we intellectually owe so much to articulation, even though the focus of all articulation is conceptual with language playing only a subsidiary part in this focus . . . we can never learn to speak except by learning to know what is meant by speech. So that even while our thoughts are of things and not of language, we are aware of language in all our thinking (so far as our thinking surpasses that of animals) and can neither have thoughts without language, nor understand language without understanding the things to which we attend in such thoughts.'[2]

At the 'top' of such a hierarchical principle there must lie some free but self-motivating agency which we might call the 'self' or the 'mind'. We might say that the brain constitutes a necessary but not sufficient condition for possession of a mind, and certainly the activity of the mind depends upon the necessary agency of sight, hearing, touch, taste and smell. My perception of the world depends upon my senses, but my senses do not determine where I go, what I attend to or what decisions I make. When man formulates a sentence he does not think one word at a time, not knowing where he is going before he gets there. He thinks in whole concepts which he then articulates in a linearised, linguistic form. Such a form can only operate at full strength if those who read or hear it are prepared to attempt to reverse this process and reconstruct through indwelling and tacit integration the whole meaning indicated by sentences. The fact that skills are involved in articulation stems from the impossibility of describing in words how our thoughts and words are related. This, and the associated skill of interpreting the words of others, leads Polanyi to summarise the relation as follows:

'. . . just as, owing to the ultimately tacit character of all our knowledge, we remain ever unable to say all that we know, so also, in view of the tacit character of meaning, we can never quite know what it implied in what we say.'[3]

35

The process of dual control has an adverse side, however. A creature possessed of the use of language may derive immense benefit therefrom, but the danger is that the very economy and availability of the written word leads him to overlook its inevitable inadequacies as an articulation of his deepest thoughts. Such convenience leads the formalisation to be treated as an absolute criterion of authority, and the attempt may even be made to find an axiomatic basis for it. The written text is available to anyone able to read it, regardless of whether he shares the non-formal interpretative framework necessary to prevent its distortion. If alien frames of thought are brought to bear upon it, the so-called axiom set, since it cannot but be inappropriate in such a framework, may appear awkward, contrived, or simply wrongheaded. Torn away from its intuitive interpretative ground, the system is open to ridicule which may itself become articulated as an opposing system denying, on the basis of the inadequacy of the formalisation, the credibility of the non-formal system it reflects.

Such invalid abstraction and misinterpretation of a formal system are almost inevitable wherever language is used. It is precisely the unformalisability of the relationship between the text and its true interpretative framework that renders logical adjustment of the situation impossible. In every learning process we are compelled to impose boundary conditions upon the necessary data, and our facility for doing this properly relies upon integrative powers derived from (inarticulate) indwelling of a community orientated towards the real ground of the formalisation.

This is immensely important when we come to interpret the Bible and the records of the past. All alien thought-worlds can be brought into service, but only a thought-world acquired in integrity and a sense of obligation to the reality of God will be appropriate.

We may illustrate the place of necessity and sufficiency by considering the popular claim that doctrinal correctness is unnecessary for the Christian. It is argued, rightly, that knowing a lot of doctrine does not make us Christians. This is a restatement of the fact that the formal without the non-formal is liable to be not only hollow, but misleading. But teaching doctrine, if accompanied by the intention of the pupil to use it to reach its focal meaning rather than rest content with formal subsidiaries, provides a necessary basis without which the Christian can scarcely grow, much as he cannot grow without physical and chemical feeding. How a Christian achieves such 'whole' awareness is unspecifiable; there are no recipes for conversion. Doctrine, we might say, is necessary, but not sufficient.

The Community of Interpretation

We are now familiar with the dual process whereby the Church sets boundary conditions over its necessary ingredients, and those ingredients provide food and guidance for the growth and life of that Church. We must now ask how the Church achieves its aim of precluding erroneous interpretations.

In a subsequent discussion of the teacher-pupil relationship we shall examine interpretative depths derivable from personal encounters, but most interpretative problems arise from the writings of men long dead. The authors of the New Testament were expressing formally their non-formal faithful understanding of the person and work of Christ. But Polanyi himself wrote:

'The words I have spoken and am yet to speak mean nothing: it is only *I* who mean something *by them.* And, as a rule, I do not focally know what I mean, and though I could explore my meaning up to a point, I believe that my words (descriptive terms) must mean more than I shall ever know, if they are to mean anything at all.'[4]

In the case of the individual pioneer this richness of meaning derives from the inevitable inadequacy both of his own perception of the significance of his discovery, and of his expression of it. Here we must note that Polanyi's understanding precludes our defining valid interpretation solely in terms of *exploring what the author consciously meant.* The personal passion of the author led him to write things of which he was himself scarcely able to perceive the meaning. To focus this process of communal interpretation, let us consider this conference as an exercise in mutual education and correction, as a small conviviality setting its own standards. If we set aside the fact that some of us knew Polanyi during his lifetime, our sole source of information about his thought comes from his own self-confessed inadequate formalisations of it. From his books the speakers and participants in the conference have derived certain impressions of his thoughts which they have integrated into their world-views. The purpose in having speakers is that we cannot all study the same things in the same depths, so we choose people who have made special studies of areas of interest to present their understandings to us, a kind of distillation of Polanyi's work amalgamated with their own views. The formalisations of the speakers in the form of words are then supplemented by a host of imponderable factors associated with human interaction. Thus together, by cross-questioning each other with the focal purpose of discerning the truth, we can supplement our text-book knowledge by what might rather dangerously be called a 'human factor'. By so doing we hope to come to a consensus or communal mind which, having taken time and effort to seek for the truth, may legitimately set its own standards within the limited horizons presently available. If we make the effort to translate all this into the sphere of the Christian Church, with its specialists, books, preachers and teachers, plus all its indescribable community aspects, we can see how the Church acts as a kind of macroscopic conference, the difference – which cannot be overlooked – being that it believes that in worship and prayer it has access to the self-revelation of the *living* God. The value of this conference will likewise not be reducible to the contents of the papers given, although these provide a necessary basis for discussion; the participants will exercise control over the subject-matter presented and contribute 'human factors' of their own in such a way as to make the whole understanding we hope to achieve far greater than could have been achieved by the sum of our separate parts. The result is that we each hope to take away from the conference an understanding of Polanyi's thought which goes beyond the mere words spoken.

At this point I must outline a serious difficulty the solution to which I can do no more than sketch in brief. We are all aware that on any one formal basis there may be erected a number of different interpretative systems. Moreover, the status of the formal material itself may be disputed, for example in differing doctrines of biblical inspiration. What are we to do if opposing systems of thought can each support themselves · from within a conviviality convinced of their mutually exclusive truths? The possibility of a plurality of positions arises because no text is sufficient to impose its own boundary conditions. Were it so able it would define a unique system of interpretation without the need for personal agencies, and mathematics is often considered to be an attempt to achieve precisely this. But as soon as we admit the unformalisability of the relationship between concepts and our articulation of them, a skilful, tacit, personal coefficient, we must accept that such a unique system is impossible.

Note that we are not implying that a text has *no* correct interpretation, but that the text itself, the formal material, is insufficient to define it. Correct readings of a text (or scientific evidence etc.) rely upon qualities of a personal nature, skills which we can acquire only by indwelling the ground which gave rise to the texts themselves. The unformalisability of the skills involved in indwelling and tacit integration renders logical and impersonal arbitration between incompatible systems impossible. This is why Polanyi admits that elements of personal confrontation and even animosity can result from such situations.

This raises the whole problem of subjectivism as it relates – or, rather, does not relate – to Polanyi's thought. He himself was aware of the charge that his system was solipsistic, but repeatedly denied it. Instead he chose, with utter consistency, to stress the purely personal character of the safeguards which prevent personal knowledge from slipping into subjectivism. These are the qualities of a sense of integrity, and obligation to the truth as the man of integrity perceives it. Integrity and obligation are qualities of the responsible man who perceives his calling to search for the truth and state his findings governed by his awareness of the transcendent perspective. This is what Polanyi meant by:

'The freedom of the subjective person to do as he pleases is overruled by the freedom of the responsible person to act as he must.'[5]

Every evaluation of a system of thought is a personal act; there are no impersonal standards. Thus the integrity and obligation of every individual in every situation counts towards the collective accrediting of a system. All we can indicate is the interpretative power and necessity of indwelling as a prerequisite, but by no means a guarantee, of finding the truth.

For example, such a plurality arose in the fourth century over the *homoousion* clause of the Nicene creed. In the dispute between those who rejected a non-biblical term and those prepared to supplement biblical terminology in the light of a richer understanding, we can see that the differences arose because of arguments over the sufficiency of the biblical formalism, whereas the Arian controversy was a dispute about the focal meaning attested by the biblical witness. The victory of the *homoousion* camp was thus a victory for the ongoing interpretative power of the Church over against misinterpretation and rudimentary literalism.

These remarks re-emphasise the impossibility of doing valid theology without believing. From an objective, detached standpoint all we *can* be is some form of literalist since we must deny the reality of the creative ground of theology in the living God. But this and all literalism deny the personal address of God to man in the Incarnation. That God chose to become man and address man personally is itself an indication of the essentially personal nature of Christian knowledge.

Faith and Life

We have now laid careful foundations for an examination of the reorientation in Christian conviction and confidence made possible by Polanyi's work. We have borne in mind his analysis of thought and speech; his insistence upon our capacity to assess our own formalisations; his description of dual control; and the difficulties of unambiguous communication. What can we infer from our findings?

The Christian disciple must be both learner and teacher; he is thus involved in the problem of interpretation and of articulation. His attempts may sometimes lead both to fumbling and pioneering. Most important of all he will need a non-formal conceptual framework with which to constrain and interpret the formalisations of others. To guide and sustain such a framework he will value the community and authority of the Church.

The mention of 'authority' leads us to a significant difference between, say, theology and mathematics. Whilst ineptitude may lead the mathematics student to believe false results to be true, the strict criteria of validity involved will preclude long-term error. Mathematical authority thus achieves a degree of impersonality once basic assumptions are agreed. (I would seriously contest the claim that complete impersonality can be achieved, but cannot discuss that here.) In theology, however, the temptation is for every Christian to claim authority for himself – but this is quite out of keeping with Polanyi's position. The great pioneer who stands over against the community in order to reform it is the exception not the rule. In most cases the shared consensus of the community of faith is the only legitimate arbitrator. The authority of the community thus amounts to its collective accrediting of the shared conceptual framework of every individual, a framework which governs the basic language of theology, and determines the legitimacy of long-term or novel innovations. It is thus clear that the communal equivalents of integrity and a sense of obligation to the truth depend crucially on the openness of the community in worship and prayer to the final criteria imposed by God himself.

Such 'accrediting' is a parallel of the appropriation of language by

40

a child, or the responsible description of reality by the scientist. Novel innovations of pioneers, unless accredited by the community, do not constitute part of the legitimate language of theology. However, genuine pioneers may recognise that such 'accrediting' will not occur during their own lifetime.

Discovery. The failure of the mathematician usually results from his inability to envisage new conceptual frameworks; it may also derive from a manipulative inability. Whilst learning results derived by others the possibility of teaching and correction exists, but for the great discoverer working on the boundaries of current knowledge there is no such possibility. Such a pioneer may often find that his symbols and his conceptual grasp begin to drift apart – what Polanyi calls the *domain of sophistication.* Either his manipulations outreach his understanding, or he finds that his visionary conceptions require mathematical tools which are not yet available. Moreover, when he makes a discovery he is likely to be the only person qualified to assess its value. In other words, only someone who brings with him a conceptual framework appropriate to an area of study and is sufficiently flexible to be moulded by new innovations is qualified to assess results in that area. Contemporaries of the pioneer may see the importance – even the profound importance – of his results, but in the end, if they should reject his results, he alone is left to decide whether to persevere with them or start again, convinced of their worthlessness by his sceptical colleagues. This is an example, whether it be in mathematics, theology, science or anything else, of the paradox of self-set standards when it impinges most crucially upon the life of the individual, a paradox which may lead the individual to a stance where his contemporaries fail to follow him, fail to accredit his findings, and yet where he persists with his views.

The theologian least of all can ignore this possibility, the possibility that the individual may be right and the majority wrong. The profound thoughts of great men may receive better appreciation from non-specialists because their minds are less moulded by erroneous concepts, although this is not to deny the possibility of real and proper criticism by peers. Jesus' reception from the 'theologians' of his day when compared with the response of his disciples shows that whilst unable to perceive the full significance of his person, they were at least able, in their simple way, to perceive that he was more important than their humdrum lives.

But what happens in the 'happy moment' when the light dawns?

Suppose someone has been groping towards the solution to a problem when suddenly, quite out of the blue, something 'clicks' – rather as when the last tumbler in a safe-lock rolls into place and the door opens. The power of such a 'click-point' is not only that it provides a solution to the problem being considered, but that it frequently falls into place as the king-pin of a whole range of associated problems and concepts. It is the quest for such moments of discovery that drives us on, the search for the 'Eureka moment'. Such discoveries are usually accompanied by the urge to share the new-found knowledge. When he tries to achieve such communication the discoverer will often begin by sharing the moment when the 'click' occurred. This may have been a chance phrase, a picture, a sentence in a book, or from no apparent stimulus at all, because our appreciation of a stimulus depends upon the framework we bring with us which, if suitably orientated or if suitably malleable will allow the chance remark to 'resonate'. Just as, for this reason, some books mean so much to some people and so little to others, the discoveries of great thinkers may or may not 'resonate' in receiving minds. His discovery may be received with 'isn't that obvious', 'don't be ridiculous' or blank incomprehension. *His* whole mental vision has been fused together into a multi-dimensional whole by a remark or clue which resonates with it; his lesser contemporaries, or even his peers, tuned in to different frequences, may fail to appreciate it at all. There is no resonance because the framework which renders the stimulus meaningful is lacking. (Try explaining relativity theory to a non-scientist.) Thus only communities with shared experiences can hope to appreciate one-another's insights, and communities with divisions will fail to accredit one-another and run the risk of dismissing profound results as truisms or nonsense. The ability of a chance remark to 'spark off' a 'click-point' does not imply that all discoveries are simply summations of individual facts. All learning, from child to genius, involves making sense of particulars (which are necessary stimuli) in a way not reducible to those (insufficient) elements. When such an integration occurs it produces a non-formal framework whose stability and richness far outweigh the formal components from which it was derived; it achieves flexibility, the capacity to cope with opposing evidence and assimilate or reject new data. Yet if we permit our children to grow up without the rudimentary framework which renders such stimuli meaningful they may fail to achieve the rich integrations we have achieved, the richest of all of which is the confrontation with the person of Christ.

Discipleship involves interpretation and communication. Both processes involve the attempt to transfer a multi-dimensional framework from one mind to another. This transference can take place only via some means of formalisation. But the formal signals we can interpret may not be co-extensive with the formal signals the teacher can control. A large part of the educational process is an attempt to enable pupils to acquire the unformalisable skills exhibited by the teacher, to make integrative leaps based upon necessary information, and to exercise control over the data in a coherent way without which it would lack ultimate meaning. We seek to inspire pupils to make leaps across logical gaps. Not only our words, but our bodily posture, our vocal inflexion, and the whole impression our being makes on the pupil involve complex formalisations of ourselves which lie in part beyond conscious control. Yet since the pupil indwells the whole being of the tutor he relies upon indwelling subsidiaries across the whole range of consciousness and unconsciousness and integrates them all together to form his focal impression. Any lack of confidence or conviction must be detected by an astute observer, and the impossibility of even the finest actor sustaining a deception over a long period of time thus accounts for my concern to re-establish a really sound framework of Christian thought freed from the destructive doubts instilled into us by adverse criticism. What we believe in our hearts will show forth in our lives, for good or ill.

The requisite multi-dimensional transference is facilitated by personal teaching far more than a purely formal (e.g. book) method. Our words, despite meaning far more than we can ever tell, become infinitely richer when imparted by the whole personal participation of a human encounter. (Why else do students still travel the world to 'sit at the feet' of thinkers whose books are readily available?) And the inevitable ambiguity of our words is lessened when the complex formalisations of committed persons constrain or exert boundary conditions upon their interpretation.

Language without a non-formal interpretative framework is essentially one-dimensional in its non-poetic forms. To impart a multidimensional conceptual whole in terms of language is thus virtually impossible. *The* theological problem regarding language is that of saying many things at once. In the Incarnation God resolves this problem by addressing man personally, and living the life of perfect unity between outward form and inner conviction.

The pioneer dwells in his area of interest, the disciple dwells in the

43

person of his master, and the members of a community dwell in each other. The discovery of Christ, discipleship of Christ and the community of Christ all hinge upon the profundity of what we have called a 'multi-dimensional' personal encounter. Polanyi uses 'indwelling' to describe entering into an intimate relationship with something or someone in which the whole life of the person concerned is involved. Indwelling is thus inseparable from commitment, and commitment is akin to love.[6] Entering into a loving relationship means committing ourselves to a future which goes beyond our understanding, and yet to which we are passionately devoted. With another person such love involves a change in both parties concerned. Despite the attitudes we bring with us which allow the first encounter to resonate, subsequent sharing will involve alteration of both parties. Love involves not only a 'click-point' which renders the mental understanding whole; it also makes us aware of possibilities beyond our comprehension. Great scientists are persuaded of the importance of their work because they love it, and perceive its importance in its rich and diverse implications. Polanyi wrote:

> 'Here in the practice of skill and connoisseurship the art of knowing is seen to involve an intentional change of being; the pouring of ourselves into the subsidiary awareness of particulars, which in the performance of skills are instrumental to a skilful achievement, and which in the exercise of connoisseurship function as the elements of the observed comprehensive whole'.[7]

The decision to commit ourselves, whether to an area of study, a line of research, or to another human being for a lifetime as man and wife, involves unformalisable skills in which we seek to evaluate untold and untellable riches. But this indescribable action is not arbitrary:

> 'It is the act of commitment in its full structure that saves personal knowledge from being merely subjective. Intellectual commitment is a responsible decision, in submission to the compelling claims of what in good conscience I conceive to be true. It is an act of hope, striving to fulfil an obligation within a personal situation for which I am not responsible and which therefore determines my calling.'[8]

Submission before the given-ness of reality is the key to truth. We are not concerned with what might have been, but with what *is*; it may not please us, and it may leave us with as many problems as when we began, but intellectual integrity and obligation will not permit us to deviate from what *is* in favour of what we would like to be.

But if knowledge depends upon indwelling, how are we to know which frames of reference to indwell before we understand them? And how far ought we to allow ourselves to be 'taken over' by a thought-world before we begin to assess its validity? Part of the answer to the first question is given by the role of the disciple as teacher and advocate. Personal advocacy of a particular way of life incorporates a range of arguments beyond conscious control which may help someone to make a decision, to obtain a 'click-point'. The impossibility of writing a recipe for such discipleship follows from the tacit components of being true to oneself and Jesus Christ, and of striving as a disciple towards wholeness of faith and action.

The second question may be illustrated by an example. If we saw someone building a Norman or Gothic arch it would be nonsensical to insist that before they complete the job they demonstrate the strength of the arch by showing us that it could stand up before completion. Until the keystone, the 'click-point', is inserted it has no strength, and threatens always to crash into chaos. But if we allow the builder to complete his work we will be able to assess its true strength. Whilst we cannot force someone to listen to our words, our formalisations of our faith, in order to show the strength of the whole, as disciples living out from a centre derived from our passionate quest for, and commitment to, truth we may influence them by a host of personal factors which do impinge upon them as wholes.

The personal community of the Church acts by each of us conveying a vast field of conscious and unconscious impressions which others integrate to a focal meaning even when they refuse to listen to or read our words. Our responsibility as disciples is to be ourselves convinced to the roots of our being in order to eliminate as far as possible all adverse unconscious expressions of our inmost feelings and doubts. To illustrate this in the heart of the Church, let us consider finally the relationship between the family and the raising of the Christian child.

The children of Christian parents naturally indwell the parental atmosphere and constantly integrate together their conscious and unconscious perception of their parents' attitudes and words. As with the disciple, if the parents have lost the inner conviction of the truth of the gospel, or if they are worried by doubts derived from the books and teachings of sceptical academics, such doubts will almost inevitably influence the child. The parents, without denying or expressing doubts about such truths verbally, may simply avoid mentioning them.

Stories imparted from youth upwards in previous generations are lost, and the non-formal world of thoughts associated with them can only with great difficulty be regained. Instead of providing basic Christian teaching at home by word and example, parents increasingly rely upon Sunday Schools to provide such teaching, but without the basic framework of thought derived from family life the Sunday School can hardly make any impression at all. The teacher is like a visionary attempting to communicate his vision to a public with no conception of what he is talking about.

There is no simple or easy way out of this dilemma. Parents cannot suddenly put on a new face, or adopt a new attitude overnight so that their faith rises up from the centre of their being. The crisis of ignorance which may beset us in a few years must be averted by attacking the crisis of credibility on a wide front across academic, educational and parochial worlds. Despite many difficulties which can be foreseen, Polanyi's thought indicates a way whereby we can rely upon our non-formal, intuitive understanding of the Gospel to be flexible enough to enable us to cope with adverse criticism. We must each be discoverers convinced of the crucial importance of the framework entrusted to us, and prepared to advocate it both consciously and unconsciously by the dedication of our lives to the service of Christ in discipleship.

When we study for examinations we attend both to details of fact and overall pictures of what is going on. When we enter the examination room we are armed with both such facts and the framework into which they fit. To obtain such a framework we need the facts, but to make coherent sense of the facts we need the framework. To answer questions set in ways over which we have no control we must be flexible in our framework in order to mould the facts to the evidence and answer required. Months or years later we will have forgotten the facts, but the framework and the flexibility will remain. The skill factor outlives the particulars, but without the particulars we could never have obtained the skill.

In the Church we are not concerned to produce congregations of biblical scholars or dogmatic theologians; we are concerned to impart the knowledge of Jesus Christ which can be received as his own personal encounter. Our efforts are necessary, but not sufficient to enable others to obtain an understanding of Jesus and the Triune God, and thereby to find life more meaningful, richer and less puzzling. A purely formal education which remains formal is susceptible to any attack which can destroy formal evidence, but by enabling people to acquire the non-formal skills of the Christian life we provide them with an indelible character, a character with which they can never be separated from the love of God. Knowledge of God is personal, and personal knowledge is not made, but discovered. Personal knowledge comes from love, and love never fails. Love cannot be described, and relies upon no formal treasures which moth and rust can corrupt. The process by which the child acquires such knowledge unconsciously must be followed by application of effort in the adult. By taking up the Bible and doctrines of the past into ourselves, and accrediting and reaffirming what we find expressed there ourselves, not because it is there but because we perceive it to be true, we find ourselves in continuity with a great crowd of witnesses living and departed who have searched for and in some degree found the love of God. From our personal knowledge of him we need not be strait-jacketed by Bible or doctrine or Church, but can argue on the basis of our non-formal perception shared with the conviviality of the Christian community, dependent upon the past, but not determined by it.

The crisis of credibility boils down to the crisis felt by each individual. People with a simple faith, that most precious of gifts, need to be told, and can be told, that their faith is legitimate, that the assaults of the sceptic are not to be feared. Certainly we may learn from biblical critic, philosopher and scientist, but the faith we have is in One who is beyond man's understanding, who is indescribable in man's words, and whose being and truth cannot be undermined by man's words. Thinking of him in a way appropriate to the way he is must take us beyond thoughts which can be spoken of adequately.

The personal encounter of man with Christ or the encounter of a scientist with the universe is an encounter in love, trust and obligation wherein he is called, and perceives the call, to relinquish the freedom of the subjective person to believe as he likes, and the freedom of the objectivist to refuse to believe at all, in favour of the freedom of the responsible person to believe as he must. His response will be to share his vision with others, a vision which he must describe despite its indescribability, a vision which he will seek to brighten by learning from similar descriptions of others, despite their inevitable inadequacy. Sharing in the community of faith which sets and confirms the standards by which we dare attempt to formalize that which lies beyond all formalism, the Christian, be he scientist, philosopher or layman, relies ultimately on the one person of Jesus Christ who said,

'If you dwell in me, then you are truly my disciples, and you will know the truth, and the truth will set you free'.

NOTES TO CHAPTER 2

1. Michael Polanyi and Harry Prosch, *Meaning*, 1975, pp. 69ff
2. *Personal Knowledge*, p. 101
3. *Personal Knowledge*, p. 95
4. *Personal Knowledge*, p. 252
5. *Personal Knowledge*, p. 309
6. *Personal Knowledge*, p. 64
7. *Ibid.*
88. *Personal Knowledge*, p. 65

3

CONVERSION AND PENITENCE

JOHN BARR

One of the curious features of Church life today is that, on the whole, 'conversion' is expected outside the Church. It was expected in the great rallies of Dr Billy Graham and his colleagues. It has its place in small sects and in congregations whose theology is conservative but in general 'conversion' does not seem to be expected as part of the normal life of the Church in Britain today.

Professor Barclay was moved to plead 'that the Church should rediscover that conversion is its business and should not be content to leave conversion to the special mission and the special evangelist'.[1]

Let us use the work of Michael Polanyi to throw light on (a) what is happening in Christian conversion and on (b) the Church's role in this. We will find particularly helpful Polanyi's teaching on (i) discovery, (ii) tacit knowledge, and (iii) communication.

Michael Polanyi and scientific conversion

Polanyi himself uses the word 'conversion'[2] for the new way of looking at the world that is part of the process of scientific discovery. A historian of science, Thomas Kuhn, also makes frequent reference to scientific 'conversion'.[3] While debate on his theory of scientific revolutions will continue[4], it is evident that he shares considerable common ground with Michael Polanyi. Both have stressed the personal contribution of the discoverer in discovery.

Let us examine the pattern of discovery as it emerges in Polanyi's *Science, Faith and Society*.[5]

Scientific discovery in 'Science, Faith and Society'

How do we make scientific discoveries? How do we move from one way of looking at the world to a better way of seeing it? How do

49

we undergo a scientific conversion? This is a problem. As Polanyi says 'There are no strict rules by which a true scientific proposition could be discovered and demonstrated to be true'.[6] But there is a pattern. It may be summarised as follows:

(1) a scientist is trained in a tradition
(2) he is disturbed by problems unsolved by tradition
(3) he has faith that he can find a solution to the problem of his choice
(4) he undertakes research passionately, conscientiously and responsibly
(5) intuition leads to the moment of vision in which he sees the world in a new way
(6) he may encounter resistance as he seeks to share his vision with others
(7) he has faith that ultimately the scientific community will recognise what is true in his work
(8) if his work is authentic it will have within it the seeds of as yet unrecognised truths
(9) the most advanced science is still limited and in need of correction.

Let us now look more closely at each step listening to what Polanyi has to say.

1. *The role of tradition.* Scientific conversion, a new way of experiencing the world, begins where we are, with the experience we already have. We all possess some kind of tradition. Polanyi points out that a young scientist is given a long and painstaking initiation into the science of his day.[7] He must absorb this tradition while at the same time retaining a critical, questioning mind.[8]

2. *Problems and perplexities.* The trigger that sets in train the process of scientific conversion is often a puzzle or perplexity or problem or anomaly.[9]

3. *The faith of a scientist.* As we are reminded so powerfully in the opening paper by Professor Torrance[10], Polanyi repeatedly emphasises that all scientific research is rooted in faith; in the belief 'that truth exists'[11] and in belief in the premises of science.[12] As he says, 'No one can become a scientist unless he presumes that the scientific doctrine and method are fundamentally sound and that their ultimate premises can be unquestioningly accepted. We have here an instance of the process described epigrammatically by the Christian Church Fathers in the words: *fides quaerens intellectum*, faith in search of understand-

ing'.[13] There is further the faith that the problem chosen for research is a 'good' problem, i.e. that it is within the powers of the scientist to solve the problem and the solution is worth while.[14]

4. *Passion, conscience and responsibility.* Across the years Polanyi repeatedly drew attention to a strange phenomenon, namely that non-scientists were selling to the world a picture of science that was inaccurate. The idea of a detached unemotional intellect solving problems with cold logic is not true to the experience of a research scientist. Out of his own practical experience Polanyi paints a different picture. The research scientist 'far from being neutral at heart, . . . is himself passionately interested in the outcome. . .'.[15] The 'love of science' is a recurring phrase in Polanyi's writings.[16] But his work is a matter of conscience. 'The scientist takes complete responsibility for every one of (his) actions and particularly for the claims which he puts forward'.[17] 'Before claiming discovery he must listen to his scientific conscience'.[18]

5. *Intuition leads to vision.* In an early work Polanyi relied on intuition to bridge the gap between problem and solution.[19] He was to spend the rest of his days spelling out the nature of this intuition.[20] Every scientist will echo Polanyi's picture of long months spent in fruitless efforts, with hopes crushed by disappointments until at last 'certain visions of the truth, having made their appearance, continue to gain strength both by further reflection and additional evidence'.[21] Polanyi quotes with approval that in any branch of research four phases can be observed namely, '*preparation, incubation, illumination* and *verification*'.[22] With the moment of vision, of illumination, the world is seen in a new light. Scientific conversion has taken place.

6. *Resistance to change.* When a scientist attempts to share his discovery with others he may meet resistance. This could be because we are psychologically resistant to change in our habits of mind,[23] or because an opponent does not share the new vision and on grounds of scientific conscience must disagree.[24]

7. *Ultimate consensus.* Polanyi rightly says, 'The fundamental unanimity prevailing among scientists manifests itself – paradoxically perhaps – most clearly in the case of conflict. Every scientist feels the urge to convince his fellow scientists of the rightness of his own claims'.[25] In scientific debate 'both contestants remain agreed that scientific opinion will ultimately decide right; and they are satisfied to appeal to it as their ultimate arbiter'.[26]

8. *In touch with reality.* Polanyi has a strong personal faith that in

research we are guided 'by the urge to make contact with a reality, which is felt to be there already to start with, waiting to be apprehended'.[27] Looking for a basis for this faith Polanyi was tempted to link it with Rhine's work on extra-sensory perception[28] but later he abandoned such speculations.[29] Meanwhile he had found a surer foundation on which to build. A good theory has within it 'an indeterminate range of yet unknown (and perhaps yet inconceivable) true implications'.[30] As we shall see below, practical examples of this taken from the history of science strengthen the conviction that in our researches we are indeed in touch with something that is real.

9. *To be continued.* The most advanced science is still limited and in need of correction. When a discovery has been made and a new way of viewing nature has been achieved many questions remain to be resolved. As Polanyi puts it 'the great scientific controversies show the range of basic questions which may remain in doubt after all sides of an issue have been examined'.[31] Great discoveries are few and far between. Ordinary scientific research is a tidying up process dealing with smaller unanswered questions. To this work there is no end. To the end of our days we are 'a society of explorers'.[32]

This structure of discovery implied in Polanyi's writings is plausible. Let us test it against two examples taken at random, one from astronomy and one from engineering.

An example from astronomy – Nicolaus Copernicus

1. *The role of tradition.* Copernicus inherited the physics of Aristotle and the astronomy of Ptolemy. Ptolemy had imagined the sun, moon, planets and stars all circling the earth daily. To account for the detailed movement of the planets against the stars he incorporated (i) epicycles (each planet moving on an epicycle whose centre travelled on a circle around the earth), (ii) excentrics (e.g. the sun moving uniformly in a circle not about the earth but about a point displaced at a distance from it) and (iii) equants (the centre of an epicycle travelling with constant angular velocity not about the centre of the circle but about the equant, a point roughly the same distance from the centre of the circle as the earth but on the opposite side).[33] Copernicus mastered these and other complexities before developing his own system.

2. *Problems and perplexities.* Other influences were in the air. Buridan[34] and his pupil Oresme[35] commenting on Aristotle had raised many questions. Novara, under whom Copernicus studied at Bologna, was dissatisfied with the complexity of the Ptolemaic system.[36]

Copernicus himself cites three problems in his introduction to *De Revolutionibus Orbium Caelestium*.[37]

(i) There is need for calendar reform. 'For first, the mathematicians are so uncertain of the motion of the sun and moon that they cannot represent or even be consistent with the constant length of the seasonal year'.

(ii) There are inconsistencies in the methods of calculation used by the astronomers of his time.

(iii) But above all they fail to give a picture of the universe. 'Also they have not been able to discover or deduce . . . the chief thing, that is the form of the universe, and the clear symmetry of its parts'.

These and other anomalies set Copernicus on the quest for a better way of viewing the universe.

3. *The faith of a scientist.* It is significant that Copernicus spent some time studying law at Bologna. There under Novara, the professor of Astronomy, he was introduced to the Pythagorean tradition and acquired the faith that the universe is to be conceived in terms of simple mathematical relationships.[38] In that faith he attempted to simplify the complex system of Ptolemy.

4. *Passion, conscience and responsibility.* Koestler has pictured Copernicus as a submissive weakling.[39] However let Copernicus speak for himself of his scientific conscience. 'For I am not so pleased with my work that I take no account of other people's judgment of it. And although I know that the reflections of a man of learning are remote from the judgment of the common herd, because he applies himself to seeking out the truth in all things as far as that has been permitted by God to human reason, nevertheless I consider that opinions which are totally incorrect should be avoided'.[40]

5. *Intuition leads to vision.* Copernicus, dissatisfied with the astronomy of his day, tells us, 'I therefore set myself the task of reading again the books of all philosophers which were available to me, to search out whether anyone had ever believed that the motions of the spheres of the universe were other than was supposed by those who professed mathematics in the schools'.[41] He explores the idea that the earth moves and goes on, 'I eventually found by long and intensive study that if the motions of the wandering stars are referred to the circular motion of the Earth and calculated according to the revolution of each star, not only do the phenomena agree with the result, but also it links together the arrangement of all the stars and spheres, and their sizes,

and the very heaven, so that nothing can be moved in any part of it without upsetting the other parts and the whole universe'.[42] This is indeed a description of a new vision and of a scientific conversion.

6. *Resistance to change* Copernicus anticipated opposition. 'Therefore, since I was thinking to myself what an absurd piece of play-acting it would be reckoned, by those who knew that the judgments of many centuries had reinforced the opinion that the Earth is placed motionless in the middle of the heaven, as though at its centre, if I on the contrary asserted that the Earth moves, I hesitated for a long time whether to bring my treatise, written to demonstrate its motion, into the light of day. . . . Accordingly as I thought it over, the contempt which I had to fear because of the novelty and absurdity of my opinion had almost driven me to suspend completely the work which I had begun'.[43] In fact he delayed full publication for over thirty years. His fears were well founded. Later Tycho Brahe, the great observational astronomer, repudiated the Copernican system on scientific grounds for two reasons: (i) it was not accurate enough in its predictions, and (ii) he could trace no apparent movement of the stars as the earth moved round the sun.

Luther, and Galileo's opponents objected on scriptural and theological grounds.

7. *Ultimate consensus.* Copernicus did not live to see his life's work accepted by the scientific community. *De Revolutionibus Orbium Caelestium* was published in 1543, the year of his death. More than a century would pass before a revised version of the Copernican theory became established as a satisfactory description of the solar system.

8. *In touch with reality.* Bishop Osiander in his preface to *De Revolutionibus* does his utmost to suggest that the hypotheses of Copernicus are merely aids in calculation and bear no relation to reality.[44] Copernicus on the other hand in his own preface is consistently claiming that, novel though it is, his description of the universe does mirror reality.[45]

Polanyi in *Science and Reality*[46] examines what it was that made Copernicus feel he was in touch with reality. Ptolemy had used epicycles, excentrics and equants as mathematical aids, and subsequent astronomers used different combinations of these as they sought increased accuracy. But such changes didn't affect the system as a whole.

For Copernicus it was different. By viewing the planets from an earth that moved around the sun he could explain 'planetary loopings by a theory which, when introducing the actually observed periods and amplitudes of oscillations, predicts a plausible sequence of orbital radii'.[47] The Copernican theory itself thus appeared to reflect reality. But Polanyi sees further vindication of this in history. That Kepler could build on Copernicus and reach his three planetary laws and that Newton could build on Galileo and Copernicus and predict Kepler's laws from first principles suggests strongly that we are approaching something real.

9. *To be Continued.* Copernicus had taken one small but decisive step forward, but at a considerable cost. Professor Butterfield sums it up thus. To follow Copernicus, 'you had to throw overboard the very framework of existing science, and it was here that Copernicus failed to discover a satisfactory alternative. . . . Once we have discovered the real character of Copernican thinking, we can hardly help recognising the fact that the genuine scientific revolution was still to come'.[48]

Even the best theory in science has much in it that will be re-written at a later date.

Now let us take an example from our own age.

Sir Frank Whittle's invention of the aero gas turbine jet engine[49]

1. *Tradition.* Frank Whittle was trained as a mechanical engineer at Cranwell and Cambridge. He was aware of the prevalent opinion, based on experience, that there was little future for the constant pressure gas turbine.

2. *Problem.* As a Flight Cadet at Cranwell in 1928 Whittle wrote an essay on future developments in flying. At that time the reciprocating aeroengine driving a propeller was the common method of powering an aircraft. This has limitations. A conventionally designed propeller is limited to speeds below 700 mph. Whittle discussed the possibility of jet propulsion, and separately, of gas turbines.

3. *Vision.* It was eighteen months later when on an Instructors' Course at the Central Flying School, Wittering, that he conceived the idea of using a gas turbine for jet propulsion. A rocket is propelled by the reaction of a jet of hot gases. But a gas turbine produces, as waste, a vast quantity of hot gas. If the efficiencies of compressor and turbine could be improved by careful design and development and if the exhaust gases could be used to propel the aircraft, a new aeroengine would be possible which would open up a new era in flying.

4. *Resistance.* Although he applied for his first patent in January 1930 Whittle received little encouragement. He submitted his ideas to the Air Ministry but was turned down on the ground that, as it was a

gas turbine, the practical difficulties in the way of development were too great. Aeroengine manufacturers were uninterested.

5. *Faith.* But Whittle himself believed it could be done. There was a curious tendency among turbine designers to believe that the low efficiencies of turbines and compressors were inevitable. He did not share this pessimism. He believed that big improvements in these efficiencies were possible. He also recognised that there were favourable factors in an aircraft application namely the low temperature at high altitude, the ram effect of forward speed, and the fact that only part of the expansion takes place in the turbine. Each of these factors helps raise the overall efficiency.

6. *Passion.* With two ex-RAF officers Whittle set up Power Jets Ltd. in March 1936 with the Air Ministry as a share holder. In every part of the design he was going beyond engineering experience. 'We were aiming at a pressure ratio of about 4/1 in a single-stage centrifugal blower when at the time, so far as we knew, a ratio of $2\frac{1}{2}/1$ had not been exceeded. We were aiming at a breathing capacity in proportion to size substantially greater than had previously been attempted. The combustion intensity we aimed to achieve was far beyond anything previously attempted. Finally, we had to get over 3,000 s.h.p. out of a single-stage turbine wheel of about $16\frac{1}{2}$ inches outside diameter, and to do it with high efficiency'.[50] The work was done on a shoe string. With the help of the British Thomson-Houston Company the first engine ran in April 1937. For the next four years Whittle and his small team worked long hours with inadequate facilities designing, testing, redesigning, testing etc. gradually improving performance and reliability until, in May 1941, the Gloster E28 flew powered by the Whittle W1 engine.

7. *Ultimate consensus.* A visit to any airport will confirm that today only very light aircraft are powered with reciprocating engines driving propellers. The gas turbine now dominates aircraft propulsion.

8. *Unforeseen implications.* Whittle did foresee with remarkable clarity many of the possible future applications. In the post-war years, at the National Gas Turbine Establishment at Pyestock, the great range of possibilities was explored in detail and followed up by aeroengine manufacturers. Today the engines powering a host of subsonic airlines and Concorde are direct descendants of the Whittle W1 engine.

9. *To be continued.* But all that lay in the future. The Whittle W1 engine was just a beginning. All over the world laboratories and test

facilities would grow up for further work on compressor, combustion chamber and turbine design and development.

Thus far we have been looking at the pattern of discovery as seen by Polanyi and illustrated from astronomy and engineering. Broadly the pattern fits remarkably well. In engineering the stages come in a different order since there the moment of vision is but the beginning of years of arduous work. Yet I suspect that for Copernicus also his initial vision was followed by the years of computations published in *De Revolutionibus*.

Now let us turn to discovery in a different field.

Michael Polanyi and our search for God

Polanyi noticed that this pattern of discovery is common to many branches of study, to mathematics, physics, chemistry, biology, medicine and he would add 'I would include also the prayerful search for God'.[51] This is well said. It stresses both the similarity and the essential difference between the physicist striving to understand the world and the Christian responding to God.

As a young research engineer my interest was in the combustion process in jet engines. In the quest for a better understanding I designed special burners which manipulated the fuel and air in ways of my choosing. But it is not for man to manipulate God. Polanyi is right to talk of 'our *prayerful* search for God'. Professor Torrance speaks of prayer in 'a relation of transcendent reference'.[52] I take this to mean reverent prayer and would agree that this is the appropriate approach to God. Is it wrong then to speak of 'discovery' as man's side of God's self-revelation? Let us look at some examples from the Old Testament.

Discovery and revelation

It would be interesting to set the experiences of say Jacob, Moses, Amos, Hosea, Isaiah and Jeremiah against the pattern of discovery that has emerged above. Time will not allow us to look at them all individually. Let us look more closely at Moses.

1. *The role of tradition.* Little Moses was a child of two worlds. In the providence of God he was brought up as a prince of Egypt and educated to be a ruler of men, but his wet nurse was his own Hebrew mother. He knew his brother and sister Aaron and Miriam. With his mother's milk he must have imbibed something of the traditions of his

forefathers. Certainly on Horeb God is 'the God of your fathers, the God of Abraham, the God of Isaac, and the God of Jacob'.[53]

2. *Problems and perplexities.* Why then should his people be slaves? What had happened to the promises made by God to his ancestors?[54]

3. *Faith.* We cannot expect a record written for a different purpose to give attention to each of the facets in our analysis of discovery. Little is said explicitly about the faith of Moses, rather it is described in practice. To use Polanyi's way of speaking, which we will meet below, on the slopes of Horeb Moses looks *from* the scene of volcanic activity *to* the God of his Fathers. This is very significant. Where primitive man would have sensed the spirit of the volcano, he is aware of the God of Abraham and Isaac and Jacob.

4. *Passion, conscience and responsibility.* Of Moses' enthusiasm for the liberation of his people there can be little doubt. He had already executed one of the Egyptian guards for cruelty to a slave.[55] But he has genuine misgivings about his own capability. The strain of having an Egyptian princess as adoptive mother and a Hebrew slave as a natural mother has left its mark. He has a speech defect.[56] Like Copernicus, Moses shrinks from facing attack. We are human and frail.

5. *Intuition leading to vision.* Moses flees for his life. He settles in Midian, marries and lives the life of a nomad. One could guess that the plight of his people lies on his heart. On the slopes of Horeb he is conscious of God's presence. To him is given the understanding that God is *Yahweh*, the Eternal[57], who is concerned for his people and who commissions Moses to set them free.

6. *Resistance to change.* Moses foresees trouble as he receives God's commission; there will be resistance both from the Egyptian authorities[58] and from his own people.[59]

7. *Ultimate consensus.* Although Moses did meet hostility again and again, today his people revere him as the founder of their nation, and Jew, Christian and Muslim look back to him with gratitude.

8. *In touch with reality.* From the human side as we watch Jacob-Moses-Amos-Hosea-Isaiah-Jeremiah-(and dare we add)-Jesus it is like watching Ptolemy-Copernicus-Kepler-Galileo-Newton-Clerk Maxwell-Einstein. Each of the Old Testament characters takes a modest step towards understanding the wonder of God.

To describe history thus is to risk being called 'Whiggish' by the historians.[60] Were one writing a full history of discovery in the Old Testament it would be necessary to follow up the failures as well as the successes, to examine the dead ends as well as the thread of continuity that runs through the history of revelation. However our aim is more modest. Polanyi describes reality in terms of unforeseen implications in our discoveries. Let us look to see if this is reflected in the pattern of discovery in the Old Testament.

Jacob advances from thinking of God as located in the family home but he does not hesitate to use practical genetics to cheat his Father-in-law.[61] There are implications in his vision not yet apparent to him which will be seen by Moses. Moses moves on to a lofty ethical monotheism in which God asks for righteousness as exemplified by the ten commandments and common law which grows out of the cases Moses has to settle. The law could all too easily lead to legalism but it has within it unforeseen implications glimpsed later by Amos in his cry for justice[62] and more fully elaborated by Jesus in the sermon on the mount. When Hosea glimpses God's forgiving love and Jeremiah suffers as God's servant there are as yet undisclosed implications which will appear to Calvary.

9. *To be continued.* God made a convenant with Moses and his people[63] but the day would come when we would look back on it, and the thousand years that followed, as the old covenant, the Old Testament, to be fulfilled and succeeded in the *new* covenant, the New Testament, made by Jesus in the upper room[64] and on Calvary.

The Bible was not written with an analysis of 'discovery' in mind. Accepting this limitation, the experiences of Moses and the others do seem to run parallel to the pattern of discovery in other fields with the significant difference that God himself is active in every stage of his self-revelation. The main difference between theology and the natural sciences is that as Christian theologians we are studying not just the creation but the Creator who reveals himself in Jesus Christ.

Some find it convenient to keep the word 'discovery' for use in natural science and 'revelation' for use in speaking of our approach to God. I wonder if there is not value in keeping both words for the two sides of both experiences? Like the head and tail of a coin they are distinguishable but inseparable. Even in natural science a breakthrough has a feeling of given-ness, of revelation. It is significant also that it is often to those who are prepared to wrestle and sweat and agonise over a problem that a solution is given. To speak of 'discovery' reflects this ,arduous labour.

We have looked at the pattern of discovery implied in the work of Michael Polanyi. We have seen this illustrated in the experience of Copernicus, Whittle and Moses. Let us now look more closely at one aspect of the pattern of discovery, at what Polanyi at first calls intuition'.

Michael Polanyi and 'intuition'

As we saw above, in his earliest analysis of the process of discovery, Polanyi was content to let something called 'intuition' bridge the gap between a problem and its solution. He was to spend the rest of his life exploring how this 'intuition' works. As he could write in the 1964 preface to *Science, Faith and Society* 'Scientific knowing consists in discerning Gestalten that are aspects of reality. I have here called this 'intuition'; in later writings I have described it as the tacit coefficient of a scientific theory, by which it bears on experience, as a token of reality'.[65] It is convenient to summarise his work in this field using illustrations from the golf course.

In the days before the cinecamera became common, the great golf professionals wrote books on how to play golf. They described carefully what they did at each stage in the swing. When eventually some of them were photographed and the cinefilm was studied frame by frame it became evident that what they were actually doing was different from what they thought they were doing. No one would dispute that these men 'knew' how to hit a golf ball. Their championship successes were proof of that. But evidently this was an inarticulate knowledge which they could not put into words. For such knowledge Polanyi coined the phrase 'tacit knowledge'.[66]

It is a common experience for a golfer to find that if he 'thinks about what he is doing' his game goes to pieces. The more he thinks about his stance, or his grip, or the backward swing, or the moment of impact the worse his golf becomes. The secret of good golf is to see clearly 'in your mind's eye' what you want the ball to do. Polanyi would see this as analogous to what happens when we recognise a face. We look 'from the features' (mouth, eyes, nose etc) 'to the face as a whole'.[67] If we concentrate on recognising a friend we are unaware of the individual features of his face. Similarly in golf when we concentrate on driving straight 260 yards down the fairway we do this 'from' our awareness of a complex combination of muscular movements 'to' the achievement of a successful drive.

Polanyi sees such *tacit knowledge* operating in the choice of a good problem, in the way an intuitive solution arises, and in the way we assess the results of experiments designed to test the suggested solution.

Now let us turn to conversion and penitence.

Conversion and penitence

Words that are good currency in one generation are apt to be devalued and become poor currency in another.

'Conversion' has suffered in this way. It is associated in some quarters with an unintellectual approach to faith. When this happens to a word it must be reminted. Let us go back to its use in scripture.

In both the Old and New Testament the basic meaning of conversion is a turning around. Thus *shubh*, *strephein* and *epistrephein* all mean either literally 'to turn' or spiritually 'to change one's ways'. In Scripture the basic idea is of 'turning to God'. For example Isaiah says:[68]

> Seek ye the Lord while he may be found,
> call ye upon him while he is near;
> Let the wicked forsake his way,
> and the unrighteous man his thoughts:
> and *let him return unto the Lord*,
> and he will have mercy upon him;
> and to our God, for he will abundantly pardon.

Again in the New Testament Peter preaches[69] 'Repent therefore, *and turn again*, that your sins may be blotted out, that times of refreshing may come from the presence of the Lord'. Penitence, *metanoia*, is basically 'thinking again' and it is a matter of experience that second thoughts often carry regret for some action or attitude in the past. As in the excerpt from Peter's sermon above, 'penitence' and 'conversion' often go together; penitence as a response of conscience, and conversion as a redirecting of the will.

The conversion of Saul of Tarsus

What light does Polanyi's picture of scientific conversion throw on the conversion of Saul of Tarsus as it is described in Acts?

1. *The role of tradition.* Saul was an orthodox Jew 'circumcised on the eighth day, of the people of Israel, of the tribe of Benjamin, a Hebrew born of Hebrews; as to the law a Pharisee, . . .'[70] Because he treated this tradition as closed he was hostile to the innovations of Jesus.

2. *Problems and perplexities.* In terms of Saul's tradition Jesus is a heretic, a convicted criminal. But something is needling Saul[71]; the courage and goodness of the martyrs are a problem.[72]

3. *Faith, passion, conscience, responsibility.* Saul has faith, passion,

conscience and responsibility in large measure but all directed in completely the wrong direction. For this reason nothing but a radical conversion, 'turning around', will suffice. This is something he could not do for himself. For this reason 'the grace of the Lord Jesus Christ' will be his theme to his dying day and beyond.

4. *Intuition leads to vision.* We made the caveat above that God is active in every stage of his self-revelation. Yet at the human level we may use Polanyi's concept of tacit knowledge to illumine what is happening. When Saul looks 'to' Calvary 'from' his tradition he sees a sinful man getting his just punishment. With the courage of the martyrs in the periphery of his vision he may have been less certain. Did looking 'from' Stephen 'to' Calvary raise questions? 'Who is this Jesus'? At what point his eyes were opened is not clear unless it was literally when Ananias layed his hands on him.[73] Only then is he able to look 'to' the cross 'from' his Damascus way experience, and the witness of Stephen and Ananias, and see Jesus in a new way. Certainly 'he is the Son of God',[74] he now proclaims in the Damascus synagogues. Here we have an interesting combination of the vertical and horizontal as Christ reveals himself to Saul. As so often in God's dealing with men, with the new outlook comes a commissioning as an ambassador for Christ[75] and Saul is baptised.

5. *Resistance to change.* Saul himself had reacted with hostility to the preaching of the Christians. With his conversion God's Word comes through Ananias, 'I will show him how much he must suffer for the sake of my name'.[76] Hostility begins at once in Damascus[77] and Jerusalem.[78] So much was this to be the pattern of his life that he could write later, 'Five times I have received at the hands of the Jews the forty lashes less one. Three times I have been beaten with rods; once I was stoned'.[79]

6. *Ultimate consensus.* Just as an authentic scientific discovery eventually finds acceptance in the scientific community, so after continuing debate, Paul's conversion experience becomes part of the Christian tradition. When later he spells out his Gospel[80] he takes it for granted that this is the gospel of the Church.

7. *In touch with reality.* Paul was indeed in touch with reality when he met Christ on the road to Damascus but, to use Polanyi's test, did this experience have within it 'an indeterminate range of yet unknown (and perhaps yet inconceivable) true implications'?[81] It certainly did. As Paul later faces the problems of young churches, for instance the congregation in Corinth, he is led to develop great spiritual principles.

Some of his words 'There is neither Jew nor Greek, there is neither slave nor free, there is neither male or female; for you are all one in Christ Jesus',[82] would take another nineteen centuries before Christians made them a way of life. After 1900 years Michael Polanyi senses that there are more discoveries to be made. 'The Bible, and the Pauline doctrine in particular, may be still pregnant with unsuspected lessons'.[83]

8. *To be continued.* The moment of vision on the Damascus road was only a beginning. Jesus was Lord, divine, the new Master of Saul's life. But what this involved needed thinking through. It would take three years in the desert and in Damascus[84] and perhaps another ten years in Tarsus before Barnabas would invite Saul to lead the Bible school in Antioch.[85]

Now let us compare and contrast sudden and gradual conversions.

Sudden and gradual conversions

Some branches of the Christian Church have taken Paul's conversion experience as a paradigm to be followed by all converts. This is a mistake.

To take another example from the golf course. I was standing with a friend on the tee of a 375 yard hole. He hit a beautiful drive, low and straight. Unfortunately on the ladies' tee in front there was a small post giving the length of the hole. His ball struck this square on and rebounded between us to travel 200 yards backwards. He had turned a 375 yard hole into a 575 yard hole! If he had continued to play that ball, as he trudged back to it, going in the wrong direction for the green, nothing but a complete turn through 180° would bring him back on to the right line. So for Paul nothing less than a complete turn around would suffice.

More often on the golf course we stray slightly. We may catch the rough or go out of bounds but it usually requires a modest change of direction to line up the second shot to the green. The New Testament term for sin, *hamartia*, means literally missing the mark, going in not quite the right direction. Both penitence and conversion have in them the thought of turning back into the difficult road that leads to life, or turning back to him who is the Way.

When a child is born into a Christian home, experiencing love in its earliest years, knowing the security that comes from a growing awareness that God cares, hearing of the love of Jesus as a tiny tot, deliberately choosing him as leader in youth, then what is needed in later life is often a series of miniconversions rather than a massive turn round. Sects who demand a Pauline conversion from everyone have somehow got it wrong. Just as wrong, however, are other branches of the Christian Church who have forgotten the need for radical conversion in any who have turned their backs on God.

It is interesting that our examination of scientific discovery leads to similar conclusions. There are from time to time discoveries in science that are so momentous that they may well be called 'scientific revolutions'.[86] In this connection Polanyi would list such names as Copernicus, Newton, Clerk Maxwell, Dalton, Darwin, Einstein etc.[87] Here the world view is changed so radically that the scientific conversion may be likened to that of St. Paul. But the greater part of scientific research is not like that. Most research is fairly humdrum, accepting the broad scientific outlook of the day but asking a small question and doing a little tidying up and consolidation. This is more akin to penitence or to what I have called 'miniconversion'.

Now let us turn to Polanyi for a final lesson.

Michael Polanyi and communication

Forty years ago my father was preaching from an incident in the life of Jesus. He had evidently done his background reading well for a member of the congregation who had visited Palestine asked him after the service, 'When did you visit the Holy Land?' When Father replied 'Never' the friend expostulated, 'But I have seen what you described and it was exactly as you said'. To use Polanyi's language, the friend had attended 'from' my Father's description 'to' life in the Holy Land and found the description a meaningful and accurate account of a reality which he had personally experienced. Polanyi calls this 'triadic communication'.[88] Professor Torrance in an essay on 'Theological Persuasion'[89] applies this to theological communication 'in which one mind directs another mind to an object by referring to it, and in which the other mind by following through the reference to the object understands the intention of the first mind'. In general, preaching is concerned with such triadic communication, the preacher pointing the congregation to God himself.

However, even in science triadic communication is often not enough to move older scientists, from a way of thought that has become established, to a new way of viewing the world. As Polanyi says, 'Demonstration must be supplemented, therefore, by forms of persuasion which can induce a conversion'.[90] A man may have to be jolted out of his set framework of ideas.

Conversion and the church

We began by drawing attention to the strange phenomenon that in Britain in the mid-twentieth century Christian Conversion was looked for outside rather than inside the Church. The Church will only rediscover that conversion is her business if Christians of all persuasions of theology have a Gospel to share. Our common aim is to turn men and women, boys and girls to Jesus Christ. How great that 'turn' must be depends on the direction in which a man is originally facing. We start with people where they are.

For a time I assisted the Rev. Tom Allan whose little book *The Face of My Parish*[91] helped mobilise the laity of Scotland in the 1950's. He used his evening services in the city centre church, St. George's Tron, Glasgow to reach out to those who had given no place to Christ in their lives. He was looking for radical conversions.

By contrast my former minister the Very Rev. George Johnstone Jeffrey excelled in helping the struggling Christian through a series of mini-conversions to a more mature Christian faith and practice. Professor William Barclay paid him this tribute in dedicating to him a volume of his daily study Bible, 'To G. J. J., Preacher of the Word, Prince of the Church, Writer of Books, whose friendship has enriched my life, whose encouragement has strengthened my effort and in whose presence I have been nearer God than at any other time'.[92]

It is the Church's task one way and another to help mankind turn to Jesus Christ. How are we to do this?

Ministry of word and sacrament

Every part of this ministry can be used to turn men to Christ. The Bible looks to our Saviour from beginning to end. The sacraments point even more directly to him. Baptism is a dramatic re-enacting of his death and resurrection. In Holy Communion we look 'from' the bread and wine 'to' his living, loving presence.

Polanyi sees worship as a potential area of discovery, 'a dwelling-place of the passionate search for God'.[93] Jesus himself encourages that search: 'Seek and you will find'.[94]

This century has seen the rediscovery of what the New Testament calls *kerygma*, the preaching that won so many for Christ in the first generation of the Church. However it is interesting to note that C. H. Spurgeon was converted through a sermon that lacked structure and content[95] but was anchored in a text pointing to Christ, 'Look unto me, and be ye saved, all the ends of the earth'.[96] The Revised Standard Version rendering is 'Turn to me. . . .'

Pastoral care

The 'turn' of conversion is not enough in itself. Accounts of evangelistic campaigns are littered with statistics of those who professed conversion and then fell by the wayside.[97] When Dr Billy Graham arrived in Glasgow he worshipped in Dowanhill Church. At the close of the service Dr Baxter invited him to address the congregation. His message was simple. 'I am glad to be here. I hope many will turn to Christ during these weeks, but I am only here for a short time. Whether these converts will go on to grow into mature Christians depends on you and the other congregations who will receive them into their fellowship'.

Even after the most thoroughgoing conversion many converts are 'babes in Christ'.[98] Babies can be very attractive but they can also be noisy, smelly, selfish little creatures. Recent converts can be troublesome at times as Paul found in Corinth. The fellowship of brother Christians and a teaching ministry are essential if the new Christian is to grow into a mature follower of Jesus Christ.

Teaching ministry

Today there is an appalling ignorance of the Christian faith. Recently I was preparing a catechumen who had up to that point never held a Bible in her hands. Experiences like that moved Professor Barclay to write that the Church must 'rediscover that her finest instrument towards conversion is teaching, teaching with such honesty, with such cogency, with such relevance, and with such evangelical devotion that the hearer is at first interested, then convinced, and finally moved to decision'.[99]

We saw that discovery does not start in a vacuum; it begins with a tradition. For the individual looking for an honest faith we must start with *his* tradition, with his past experience. We must begin where he is. Not every preacher can succeed in this from the pulpit. It is perhaps easier face to face in personal counselling or in small groups.

The value of small groups

Polanyi has shown that a young scientist learns by being in the company of an experienced research scientist and watching how he goes about his work.[100] Sitting in a Church pew once a week will not necessarily in itself enable a young Christian to share in Christian Fellowship.[101] Secular organisations that are concerned with the formation of new habit patterns (e.g. slimming clubs or Alcoholics Anonymous) find group meetings invaluable.

In the first generation of the Christian Church house-churches[102] provided a family atmosphere where 'babes in Christ' could grow up.[103] All over the world today the Church is rediscovering the value of such small groups. Living the Christian life requires practice. Just as a novice at golf can read books and listen to a professional but only truly begins to learn as he takes a club in his hands and swings it, so the convert only begins to learn 'the Way'[104] when living out his faith in the company of mature Christians. Have we perhaps been slow to expect young Christians to share their faith with others? Jesus sent out the twelve on mission[105] without waiting for them to understand his teaching. This was a necessary part of their training. Small groups are suited to this kind of work.

Prayer and the Holy Spirit

As we close let us watch the wisdom of the apostles. Their work is rooted in prayer.[106] Jesus had told them repeatedly to wait for the gift of the Holy Spirit. 'You shall receive power when the Holy Spirit has come upon you; and you shall be my witnesses. . . .'[107] He had promised earlier that prayer asking for the gift of the Holy Spirit is prayer God is eager to answer.[108]

What does this mean? Just as a piece of successful research brings a scientist into closer touch with reality so to share the gift of the Holy Spirit is to be in touch with God himself. What this will mean for us we cannot foresee – but then it is in the nature of life that a closer contact with reality carries with it undisclosed implications that will be unfolded in the future.

1. William Barclay, *Turning to God*, 1963, p. 101
2. Michael Polanyi, *Personal Knowledge*, p. 151
3. Thomas S. Kuhn, *The Structure of Scientific Revolutions*, 1962, e.g. pp. 19, 150ff, 159
4. Smithsonian Institution, 5th International Symposium, *The Nature of Scientific Discovery*, 1975, e.g. pp. 161, 394, 420, 422f, 542, 550, 567, 569ff
5. Michael Polanyi, *Science, Faith and Society*, 1946 and 1964
6. *Science, Faith and Society*, p. 58; see also p. 21
7. *Science, Faith and Society*, pp. 42ff
8. *Science, Faith and Society*, pp. 46
9. *Science, Faith and Society*, pp. 22ff
10. See ch. 1 above, pp. 8ff
11. *Science, Faith and Society*, p. 70
12. *Science, Faith and Society*, p. 76
13. *Science, Faith and Society*, p. 45; see also p. 15
14. *Personal Knowledge*, p. 124
15. *Science, Faith and Society*, p. 38
16. *Science, Faith and Society*, pp. 55, 64
17. *Science, Faith and Society*, p. 40
18. *Science, Faith and Society*, p. 55
19. *Science, Faith and Society*, pp. 29, 45
20. See below p. 85
21. *Science, Faith and Society*, p. 30
22. *Science, Faith and Society*, p. 34
23. Thomas F. Torrance, *God and Rationality*, 1971, p. 197
24. *Science, Faith and Society*, p. 51
25. *Ibid.*
26. *Science, Faith and Society*, p. 63
27. *Science, Faith and Society*, p. 35
28. *Ibid.*
29. *Science, Faith and Society*, p. 14
30. *Personal Knowledge*, pp. viif, 5, etc.; see also *Science, Faith and Society*, p. 23
31. *Science, Faith and Society*, p. 15
32. *The Tacit Dimension*, ch. 3
33. See, e.g., *The 'Conflict' Thesis and Cosmology*, 1974, AMST 283. 1-3, pp. 59f
34. Thomas S. Kuhn, *The Copernican Revolution*, 1957, pp. 118-123
35. *The Copernican Revolution*, pp. 114ff, 119f
36. *The Copernican Revolution*, p. 128
37. N. Copernicus, *On the Revolutions of the Heavenly Spheres*, 1543, trans. by A. M. Duncan, 1976, p. 25
38. Michael Polanyi, *Personal Knowledge*, p. 6
39. Arthur Koestler, *The Sleepwalkers*, 1959
40. N. Copernicus, *On the Revolutions of the Heavenly Spheres*, p. 23
41. *On the Revolutions of the Heavenly Spheres*, p. 25
42. *On the Revolutions of the Heavenly Spheres*, p. 26
43. *On the Revolutions of the Heavenly Spheres*, pp. 23f

44. *On the Revolutions of the Heavenly Spheres*, pp. 22f
45. *On the Revolutions of the Heavenly Spheres*, pp. 23-27
46. Michael Polanyi, 'Science and Reality', *British Journal of the Philosophy of Science*, 1967, vol. 18, pp. 177-196
47. 'Science and Reality', p. 185
48. Herbert Butterfield, *The Origins of Modern Science*, 1951, pp. 27, 30
49. Frank Whittle, 'The Early History of the Whittle Jet Propulsion Gas Turbine', *Proceedings of the Institution of Mechanical Engineers*, 1945, vol. 152, pp. 419-35
50. Frank Whittle, *op. cit.*, p. 420
51. Michael Polanyi, *Science, Faith and Society*, p. 34
52. Thomas F. Torrance, *God and Rationality*, p. 205
53. Exodus 3.15
54. Genesis 12.1-3
55. Exodus 2.12
56. Exodus 4.10
57. Exodus 3.14
58. Exodus 3.11, 19
59. Exodus 4.1
60. Herbert Butterfield, *The Whig Interpretation of History*, 1931.
61. Genesis 30.25ff
62. Amos 5.24
63. Exodus 34
64. 1 Corinthians 11.25
65. Michael Polanyi, *Science, Faith and Society*, p. 10
66. *Personal Knowledge*; *The Tacit Dimension*; *Knowing and Being*
67. *The Tacit Dimension*, p. 10
68. Isaiah 55.7
69. The Acts of the Apostles, 3.19, RSV
70. Philippians 3.5, RSV
71. Acts, 26.14
72. Acts 7.59f
73. Acts 9.18
74. Acts 9.20, RSV
75. Acts 22.14-16
76. Acts 9.16, RSV
77. Acts 9.23
78. Acts 9.29
779. 2 Corinthians 11.24, 25, RSV
80. 1 Corinthians 15.1-11
81. Michael Polanyi, *Personal Knowledge*, p. viii
82. Galatians, 3.28, RSV
83. Michael Polanyi, *Personal Knowledge*, p. 285
84. Galatians 1.17f
85. Acts 11.25f
86. Thomas S. Kuhn, *The Structure of Scientific Revolutions*
87. Michael Polanyi, *Science, Faith and Society*, pp. 13, 28
88. *Knowing and Being*, pp. 182ff
89. Thomas F. Torrance, *God and Rationality*, pp. 195f

90. Michael Polanyi, *Personal Knowledge*, p. 151
91. Tom Allan; *The Face of My Parish*, 1954
92. William Barclay, *The Gospel of John*, 1955, p. v
93. Michael Polanyi, *Personal Knowledge*, p. 281
94. St. Matthew 7.7, RSV
95. Ernest W. Bacon, *Spurgeon*, 1967, p. 23
96. Isaiah 45.22
97. Owen Brandon, *The Battle for the Soul*, 1960, p. 69
98. 1 Corinthians 3.1
99. William Barclay, *Turning to God*, 1963, p. 101
100. Michael Polanyi, *Science, Faith and Society*, p. 43
101. Acts 2.42
102. Acts 12.12, etc.
103. Ephesians 4.13
104. Acts 9.2, RSV
105. St. Mark, 8.7ff
106. Acts 1.14
107. Acts 1.4-8, RSV
108. St. Luke 11.13

4

CHRISTIAN AFFIRMATION AND THE STRUCTURE OF PERSONAL LIFE

DANIEL W. HARDY

A very serious gap has opened up in a central place in modern thought and life, in the dynamics of personal life and thought. We are eager enough to rescue ourselves from what we deem to be the inhuman routines of modern life, to provide conditions in which we can 'be ourselves'; but we find it much more difficult to make good use of them. Once freed from the need to rebel against the inhuman routines, or the authorities which impose them, we find ourselves unable to 'be ourselves' except by settling down in some more pleasurable routine created for us by others: we have little idea of the 'person' we want to be, except in a rather low sense of the word.

It would be interesting and profitable to explore the evidence for the vacuum which now exists in personal life and thought, but we must simply list some of it: (1) Protests against inhuman ideologies and routines encourage us to 'be ourselves' but give us no goal for our new-found freedom. (2) If we have any inkling about what to strive for, the striving is to take place in our private lives and by our own effort, independent of any ground external to ourselves. For we are responsible for finding whatever possibilities of full life there may be, and for finding our way amongst them, doing our best as we go along, even if we are dragged down in the process. (3) The basic existence to which we are thus driven has become a private, base, or primitively human one, not a fully human one. (4) We are unable to conceive of a ground for fully human life in God; we can no longer think of a fully personal existence in God.

Bringing to the fore the vacuum which now exists in the understanding of the person and its ground, and in the achievement of personhood, provides us with an important – but very dangerous – vantage-point from which to understand Michael Polanyi's thought.

The danger, of course, is that it may lead us to pervert the understanding of Polanyi by making it captive to two tendencies apparent in modern considerations of the person. In other words, we may mistake the 'personal' knowledge with which Polanyi was concerned by assimilating it to conceptions of person which are at odds with it. On the one hand, Polanyi does not share the hypothesis common to most psychotherapists, 'that it is important that each individual should be able to develop his own personality in as unrestricted and complete a way as possible',[1] even if reference to personal knowledge at first seems to suggest that. For him 'personal' refers to a responsible activity claiming for its comprehension a universal validity – an outward-directed movement toward what is to be known, and an appraisal of it which meets a commitment to universal standards – not an activity of self-development. On the other hand, Polanyi does not share the hypothesis common to many philosophers and theologians, that knowing is a personal process of interpreting reality through particular modes of experience or categories. For him 'personal' refers to the use of skilled intuition which is open to, and under the control of, reality. While he insists upon the importance of the personal, Polanyi always makes it contingent upon what is 'there' as reality and what is universally true about it. The direction and discipline of knowledge prevent its *personal* character from becoming *subjective*.

If we avoid these dangerous misinterpretations of Polanyi's views, his work can supply us with important inroads into the vacuum in the understanding of the personal. Firstly, it shows us the pattern by which we should attempt to understand the personal.

An apt illustration of the pattern which Polanyi establishes is the description by Yehudi Menuhin of a crucial event in his life. He speaks of his early experiences playing the violin – from his childhood until about 1935 (when he was about 20), increasingly nagged by the thought that he could no more explain why he played given passages as he did than *how*; despite all the expert explanations he had had from teachers, it was his ardour that carried his audience, while 'reason stood outside' as he was unable to explain and justify his particular playing. A two-week interval in his travels, on a boat travelling from Australia to South Africa, finally brought him to study one particular sonata. At the end he had come to a point where he could analyse the music, and justify reasoningly his particular performance – in the way he thereafter felt was necessary for all works he played. This is his comment:

> 'Obvious? (Menuhin says) Stating the obvious made me feel less contingent. Discerning a form glassed in its smallest constituent part, I saw myself through a mirror and thus made a first conscious step to adulthood, to analysis and synthesis, to consciousness and clarity of (in)sight. . . . My instinctive *tours de force*, the recognition accorded me, the fantasy of matrilinear descent from a martial figure, did not confirm me so emphatically as one small triumph of reason, one unaided perception of significant form. I had yet to discover its human coefficient, the shape of my individual history, the significance buried in events. . . . Still, having found internal significance in music, I found myself significant; having entered knowingly what had hitherto seemed opaque and given, I no longer beheld myself as nature's sport.'[2]

Amongst several things, what is important about this episode is the direction in which Menuhin moves to find confirmation of his significance. He does not affirm himself, but finds confirmation in his perception of significant form. There is a profound interrelation between the discerning and affirming of significant form – entering knowingly into what had seemed opaque and given – and the finding that he is significant, has meaning and purpose. To be sure both are incomplete: the analysis and discernment have to continue, and the 'human coefficient' has yet to be filled out by an awareness of his personal history and vocation. But the fact remains that personal confirmation occurs through the discerning of significant form, not the other way round: the direction is outward.

This is probably the most important feature of Polanyi's emphasis on personal knowledge, its 'outer-directedness'. And this is important not only for the achievement of knowledge, preventing it from being subjective, but for its contribution to the personal. Polanyi's emphasis on the movement of thought away from ourselves makes it clear that there is an inescapable ordering in the interrelation between the discernment of significant form and the discovery of our significance, and that the latter is achieved through the former. And it is important to recognise that it *is* achieved: the personal is not only a contribution to, but also a derivation from, knowing. But neither can knowing be made incidental to the achievement of the personal.

73

Menuhin's words reveal another aspect of Polanyi's contribution. As he shows how he analyses the Beethoven Violin Concerto, pursuing the permutations of the opening notes of the entry of the violin, he says, 'the further I pursued my inquiry, the clearer it became that these notes could not be any others'.[3] There is what he calls a 'structural norm' or 'inherent form': the music has an inner rational structure within which any interpretative variation must remain in order to be valid. Obviously, this does not cancel out the possibility of variations in individual performances, but they must not 'flout the inherent form' if they are to be valid.

Similarly Polanyi emphasises not only the necessary outer-directedness which is essential to knowledge and to the finding of personal significance, but also the intrinsic rationality of reality and the control it should be allowed over our knowing. It is not simply human creations in music, but reality itself, which has 'inherent form', a normative structure or order, and our knowing can only be valid if it is in accord with this norm. This does not 'throw itself' at us, powerfully controlling our knowing, but it is normative for us nonetheless, validating our interpretations. Knowing is not, therefore, all in man's hands; it is a dynamic quest by man, but to succeed it must conform to the inherent form of reality. Man's powers of interpretation do not reign supreme.

Now, with these considerations – this basic framework – in mind, we need to look carefully into Polanyi's account of the dynamic of knowing in order to establish its contribution to the personal. His account is intended to describe a process of life, a performance or activity in which we engage in order both to know and at the same time to be ourselves – which if we accomplish successfully will provide knowledge *and* enable us to become ourselves.

The whole activity of knowing is for Polanyi not detached theoretical contemplation, but involved, participatory practice which must, in order to succeed, be *done* with intellectual powers which must themselves be acquired, and a strategy which must be followed. The passionate participation and the intellectual powers – especially apparent in the appraisal which occurs in appreciation of order and probability (in the exact sciences) and in skills and connoisseurship (in the descriptive sciences) – are what Polanyi refers to as 'personal'. In so stressing passionate personal contribution as a vital component of knowledge, what Polanyi does is to move decisively away from the mechanical model of early modern science, where reality was seen as residing in the object or in the laws which appeared to govern the object's behaviour, and to move toward a dynamic or interactionist model, where reality is perceived in the relation between the object and its knower.

How is it that Polanyi sees that there is a personal contribution by the knower, or an involvement of the subject in knowing the object? He does so by starting 'farther back' in the knowing process and emphasising the continuing presence of factors operative there even when knowledge is achieved. So he sees the importance of imagination, intuition and appraisal – in discovering or knowing good problems, for example – where these are discounted in accounts of knowledge which concentrate on the 'finished product' of knowledge. And having seen these there, he is provided with a key for understanding the finished product which shows them there also. In other words, he concentrates on what is sometimes called 'heuristic', the intuition or questioning by which someone anticipates what is to be known and then, informed by this, goes on to specify and determine it. For Polanyi, this is always a personal process, and even the final result (a reasoned argument) bears the mark of personal contributions; these intuitions, suspicions or problems from which we start in knowing, and the discoveries which we make, do not exist without a person. 'Nothing is a problem or discovery in itself; it can be a problem only if it puzzles and worries somebody and a discovery only if it relieves somebody from the burden of a problem.'[4] The same is true for the logic and reasoning by which a discovery is validated, and for the framework in terms of which the discovery is meaningful.

The effect of Polanyi's account is to make knowing a story in which we become involved, even spellbound – which thereafter has its own unfolding sequence. Furthermore, the story is not private, but must be capable of being a story for all others; this is the 'universal intent' which the knower has for what he knows. Just this happens when Coleridge's Ancient Mariner stops the wedding guest and transforms him by the tale he tells:

> 'He holds him with his glittering eye –
> The Wedding-Guest stood still,
> And listens like a three years' child:
> The Mariner hath his will.

> 'The Wedding-Guest sat on a stone:
> He cannot choose but hear;
> And thus spake on that ancient man
> The bright-eyed Mariner'.

But Polanyi's account suggests, as we said before, not illusion – not that Coleridge did either – but active and involved knowing under the structural norm of reality, and with universal intent.

This active and involved knowing happens personally, by living in and acting by the framework and methods which we employ. It is only by this 'in-dwelling' that they become fully ours. They become natural to us, frameworks and techniques which we employ happily; they are not at a distance from us, and laboriously taken up each time we use them, but like a home in which we dwell, from which we move into the world, and with which we experience and meet the world. Though at some point they have to be acquired, and this may mean a great deal of hard work, their place is to be *seen through*, and to direct the energy of our perception or other work. Dwelling in them happily, and dwelling in them with others, gives a possibility of knowledge, of putting things in the right perspective, which is not otherwise available. If I say that 'my home is where my family is' it may show why, when I go skiing, I ski better with my family than otherwise – though, of course, I could not ski at all if I had not learned also to 'dwell' happily in that.

I must emphasise that these are not simply psychological matters with which we are dealing, though other accounts of the process suggest that they are. What we are seeing is the personal factor in seeing though frameworks and techniques to 'what is there', the personal commitment to, and indwelling of, frameworks and techniques, and the passionate wish to search through (by means of) them. And the disruption or absence of happily-indwelt frameworks and techniques can seriously undermine this 'seeing-through'. I remember, for example, being in the middle of a tennis game – playing reasonably well (for me, anyway) – and hearing in the distance the ringing of a telephone. That ringing upset my perception of the situation, and my subsequent playing – both perception *and* activity. Why? Because for days I had been so repeatedly and deeply affected by the responsibility of sorting out a difficult pastoral situation by telephone that my basic framework of understanding, as well as my perception and motor impulses, suffered a *spasm* at the ringing of that bell which in effect blocked my ability to 'see through' them to the situation at hand.

But we have not yet seen the full significance of Polanyi's view – particularly for personality. We have been seeing what has been called (by Torrance) the 'vectorial' character of knowing as Polanyi

76

sees it. What is it in this 'seeing-through' that actually sustains the frameworks and techniques and enables us to in-dwell them happily? Are we simply to acquire them, make them 'natural' to us, because such things make human beings content and happy? Or are we to acquire them because they are useful? We might then justify them on affective grounds and on functional ones. Interestingly, these are the ways in which interpretative frameworks and techniques are supposed (by many nowadays) to be justified: all alike are on the same plane, and defended because they 'feel right' or are useful (technologically, socially, personally) – it makes no difference whether one chooses to believe in the Incarnation of God in Jesus Christ or in Jesus as a maximally great human teacher, in marriage or cohabitation, in redemption as fact or as feeling, in God as a transcendent convergence-point of all human religious quests or as personal and loving, as long as it feels right or has good results.

Polanyi's view implies something quite different, through its notion of subsidiary and focal knowledge. He suggests that we must recognise two distinct kinds of awareness which occur – cooperatively, so to speak – in all knowing that we do. What we normally call knowing is a focussed act resulting in a *focal* awareness – as when we attend fixedly to something. In achieving this, however, we rely on a *subsidiary* awareness of clues, anticipations, frameworks and techniques. *Focal* awareness, when reasoned and articulate, is *explicit* knowledge; *subsidiary* awareness, which remains unformulated, is *tacit* knowledge. So, we always 'know more than we can tell', because knowing includes not only focal but also subsidiary awareness, and includes not only the explicit and formulable but also tacit knowledge.

Now, focal knowing occurs through a gathering and shaping of subsidiary knowing; there is a gathering and shaping of ourselves and our capacities which is necessary to focal knowing – and that self-shaping is a personal contribution by the knower, by which frameworks and techniques become 'natural' to us so that we dwell in them happily. But the question we have been asking is, in effect: Is this just a 'personal-utilitarian' view, in which this subsidiary knowing is gathered and shaped because it is useful affectively ('feeling right') or technologically, socially, or personally?

If the proper view of the relation between focal and subsidiary knowing is taken, the answer must be 'no': Polanyi is not what we have inelegantly titled a personal-utilitarian. The reason for this lies in the achievement of comprehension. When comprehension is achieved,

77

diffused subsidiary awareness is focussed in such a way that particular elements of subsidiary awareness are gathered in focussed awareness of a whole. Their particularity as elements does not disappear, subsidiary awareness does not disappear; but they are also seen as members of a whole through the new focal awareness which has occurred. They are no longer distributional only, but also integrative; another level of integration has supervened which endows them with a meaning. This actually affects our subsidiary awareness, and affects our 'shaping': we are not only self-shaping, but *shaped* by this new integration in focal awareness. And such a shaping can be a radical transformation, a 'conversion' which grounds our whole subsidiary awareness differently.

This is crucial for our understanding of the personal, and for the source of that happy in-dwelling of frameworks and techniques which we were discussing a moment ago. It is not only a human focussing of subsidiary awareness which occurs, but an integration through which subsidiary awareness is altered — by which a different 'subsidiarisation' occurs. And this is what *affirms* the personal indwelling of frameworks and techniques; they are not only instruments to be valued for utilitarian ends. A double affirmation takes place: focal awareness is an affirmation which integrates, but this affirmation subsidiarises elements of awareness; in doing so it affirms them as happy dwelling-places appropriate to the person who uses them and to the focussed awareness in which they operate. In other words, the integration which occurs in focussing grounds subsidiary awareness anew.

The affirmation of subsidiary awareness, and of the personal shaping by which it had been affirmed, is not a magical change but a transformation which is often slow. In cognitive awareness, it may take a long time to conform the frameworks, problems and techniques to what is affirmed by focal awareness. In awareness more broadly conceived, it also may be a long time. For example, the early history of individual human beings may condition their view of themselves so that they can see themselves as having no value; thereafter, life becomes a struggle to acquire worth, even an insatiable desire for praise. In the face of a longtime confirmation that they are of no value, occasional words and friendship will have little effect, and requests that they 'have faith', or condemnations for not trusting others or for 'being selfish', will simply reinforce that feeling of valuelessness which is so deeply entrenched. One might expect that good working and acknowledged success would undo the damage, would reverse that feeling of worthlessness. But at best, it does so only partially.

78

Or consider the reversal which many people suffer when in pain or at the time of death, their own or others': they simply cannot integrate these experiences within the framework which they have established by which they perceive their lives. Like a woman I knew who emerged from church one day to find her car dented, their response is, 'I've been in church; how could this happen to me'?

The common element in all these situations is an inability to 'subsidiarise' problematic awareness and events: they remain painful and contrary — the accrued sense of worthlessness which friendship and success cannot overcome, the pain and fear of life which seems senseless. On the face of it, an adequate 'personal commitment' to appropriately comprehensive frameworks and techniques, to a notion of the 'meaning of life' for example, would do the job — would 'work' for us personally. But such is not the case, precisely because a personal commitment of this kind could not — and does not — withstand the pressure of such extreme situations. Or, to put it differently, 'personal utilitarianism' (as we described it earlier) does not work.

Here is where the occurrence of focal awareness is so important: though it occurs as a human focussing of subsidiary awareness, it occurs as an integration through which that subsidiary awareness is *made* subsidiary — affirming elements of awareness 'in their place', putting them 'in their place' within the integration which occurs in focal awareness, even if this is sometimes only a gradual process. In other words, even though its location is in the area of personal commitment and shaping, it has an integrating 'force' which places elements of personal awareness in their right order, ordering them relative to each other and to the higher integration which has occurred.

It makes a great deal of difference of what 'order' the focal awareness is in itself, as we shall see. Certainly, the occasional words offered to one who cannot acknowledge his own value provide assurance or imperatives, but do not yield such focal awareness as could mediate integration and subsidiarisation: the fragmentation of a disturbed life remains. And in the other situation mentioned, people who confront pain and death with no suitably integrating focal awareness will see these experiences as contradictory and fearsome. What is needed is something much more encompassing, capable of bringing about a focal awareness which subsidiarises such contradictions in their 'right place' within a wider awareness of life, where withheld love, pain and death are contained in an integrating focal awareness. In such a

79

situation, they are affirmed, and their otherwise destructive energy is structured and directed productively: they do not cause a kind of cerebral or behavioural 'cramp' as if the world was turning in and scolding the human being unlovingly, but are ordered in an integrating awareness which enables work to be done and life to be lived.

What are the conditions under which such integrating focal awareness occurs? It is tempting to say that what is required is an unrelenting effort to bring about a focal awareness which will subsidiarise positive and contrary experiences. That is to suppose that the conditions for integrating awareness are produced by the effort of human interpretations – that the world is a 'vale of soul-making' in which human beings develop through their interpreting and behaving. But we have seen already that this egotistical or Promethean alternative does not – cannot – integrate and subsidiarise in ways which are adequate. A wider and more integrating locus or agency is necessary.

The contrast with what human beings can achieve through their interpreting is instructive. Their tendency is always to eradicate differences, purchasing integration by reducing differentiation. Several examples show this: the same kinds of *knowing* are supposed to be appropriate whether the 'known' is a stone or a human being. *Human beings* are grouped in stereotypes: the poor are only 'the poor', and their intrinsic dignity and individual achievement go unrecognised; the loved one is remade in the image of a mother or some 'ideal' figure. All *religious perspectives* are supposed to be comparably anthropomorphic and mythological. As these and many other illustrations might show, the tendency of human beings is, when they produce focal awareness in their efforts to interpret, to assimilate what is different into what is the same or familiar, producing an integration which eradicates differences – whether differences of knowing, being, perspective or relationship. But particularity and difference should be honoured and respected in focal awareness, not superseded.

Nor is that the only problem with human efforts to interpret. Not only do they tend to eradicate differences, they also disorder proper relationships. An episode in Pirsig's *Zen and the Art of Motorcycle Maintenance* illustrates this; it describes mechanics who had, in their attempts to fix a motorcycle, made it much worse:

'Good-natured, friendly, easygoing – and uninvolved. They were like spectators. You had the feeling they had just wandered in there themselves and somebody handed them a wrench. There was no identification with the job . . . They were already trying not to have any thought about their work on the job . . . They had something to do with it, but their own selves were outside of it, detached, removed. They were involved in it but not in such a way as to care'.[5]

Here, there is no question that the mechanics have a focal awareness produced by their interpretation of life, but it is of such a kind as to alienate them from their work, making them detached 'spectators'. That is, they have no caring relationship with their work: their relationship with it is disordered, inappropriate to what it is and what they are, and they are cut off from it so that they can live apart, in another private world. But why is this a disordered relationship? Because they are unable to give their work its due, and unable to integrate their work and their privacy.

As we saw, it is the great virtue of Polanyi's picture of knowledge that it presents focal awareness, achieved in the personal commitment of the knower to reality, as in principle capable of such subsidiarising of what is different as will not either eradicate differences or disorder relationships. His emphasis of the unspecifiable element in knowing, which comes to us in a kind of recognition, places what we know beyond our control (whether by knowledge or technology) – in effect preserving our *respect* for it. But, on the other hand, that very 'thing' which we recognize subsidiarises our knowing and grounds our personal commitment. The recognition authenticates our way of recognising and enables us to dwell in it happily: in that *we* are affirmed.

But Polanyi's picture allows also for different 'orders' of awareness, and these would bring different 'kinds' of subsidiarisation – and therefore different ways in which we are affirmed. Hence he sees different grades or types of reality which differ in the manner in which they are real, because of their range of relevance. This is like saying that they differ in their 'simplicity' where simplicity means the capacity to answer questions without appealing to other factors, or where it means the capacity to generate unforeseen discoveries. As Polanyi points out, a cobblestone is less profound than a person or a problem in the sense that the cobblestone has much less possibility of yielding interesting information or unexpected revelations, and (as we would say) a much more limited range of relevance.[6] And what follows from this is that the subsidiary knowledge (or clues) which we employ in focal awareness of a cobblestone will be subsidiarised not only differently but also less deeply than that which we employ in focal awareness of a person.

81

The old saying goes: 'It takes one to know one'. In this case, the saying might be taken to mean: a stone requires only a stone to recognise it, but a problem requires a problem-recogniser, and a person requires a person-recogniser. There is a difference not only in the grade of focal awareness in each case from the others, but also in the grade of subsidiarisation. And it is as dangerous to collapse all kinds of subsidiarisation into one as it is to collapse all forms of focal awareness into one. Furthermore, it is as dangerous to collapse into one all the orders of relationship which occur between the 'known' and the 'knower' as it is to reduce into one all kinds of focal awareness and all kinds of subsidiarisation: focal awareness, subsidiarisation and modes of relationship all clearly vary, and vary in *richness* and *fruitfulness* (or range of relevance) according to the 'object' and the 'subject', the 'known' and the 'knower'.

Clearly, however, we are never in the position of a stone when we know a stone, or of a particular form of animate life when we know that. For that reason our focal awareness, subsidiarising, and mode of relationship are a 'mixture' – 'I knowing the stone (or animal)'. We begin from a focal awareness, a recognition, which is a participation in another grade of reality. That involves recognition of the structure and organisation, and of the operation and intelligence in the case of organisms, which is characteristic of the particular 'grade of reality' which is recognised. But for things and organisms 'lower' than the knower, even if (as Polanyi says) there is a personal commitment and participation in them which cannot be dissolved into impersonal terms, the 'ordering' of this participation arises from the thing or organism known.

That is, the mode of participation is the result of a subsidiarisation which occurs through the focal awareness of that particular thing or organism. For the knower in his personal commitment, there is a voluntary self-restriction (the voluntary 'side' of the subsidiarisation) which prevents his participating in the thing or organism known in a way which might be suitable to a human being. Thus, the scientist's 'loving' attention to the object he is examining is not the same as that he gives to his spouse – or should not be; nor is the care with which someone washes a beloved car the same as that he gives his children. We might say that he is personally committed to an impersonal participation in the object's impersonal commitments: to do otherwise would be to mistake the object focally known through a mistaken participation. Yet as a human being, he has the unique possibility of doing

82

so, which is not open to lower species; he can achieve something in knowing it which it cannot.

What about 'deeper' realities than cobblestones and objects and lower organisms, those with power to manifest themselves in yet-unthought-of ways and with more unlimited relevance? If these can be 'known' in focal awareness, then they will bring a much more unrestricted participation on the part of the knower; there will be no need for self-restriction to limited participation. There is the possibility here of focal awareness which will bring a uniquely human subsidiarisation. For example focal awareness of a *person* might, through subsidiarisation, constitute the knower as a *person*.

We must be careful here to discriminate between various possibilities which may be available, because not all are likely to permit fully human subsidiarisation. It is easy to suppose that the *process* of ascending to a higher focal awareness will itself provide the possibility of a fully human participation in this awareness. There is today much emphasis placed on the desirability of 'openness' and on the search for childlike innocence, each motivated by passionate curiosity — a kind of 'transcendent eros'. But there is no reason to suppose that such an ascent, even if it represents an improvement on the consequences of lower focal awareness, will provide the possibility of fully human participation. Polanyi himself seems sometimes to suppose this — to mistake the ascent which is possible in passionate personal commitment for the formation of a fully human person which can occur through focal awareness of another person.

Other dangers arise from not discriminating the kinds of focal awareness which may occur for a human being. It is remarkably easy to stop at the discovery of a particular idea or aspect of another human being, and to make this one's focal awareness, allowing it to organise one's skills or behaviour. To focus on the appearance of another or his/her sexuality, to take two possibilities, can lead to gathering facts about him/her (which is a subsidiarised mode of relationship) or to preoccupation with the technique of sexual relationship; in such cases, absolutising particular aspects brings about subsidiarisation which is as subpersonal as is the aspect focussed upon, and the result is a wild vacillation in which the knower can achieve an ecstasy which is also an agony — an ecstasy of achievement which is also an agony of unfulfilment.

It is no bad thing to be specific in focal awareness, or to be positive in the manner in which one is related to what is known: these are not the problem in the cases just mentioned. The problem arises when these specific and positive aspects take on all-encompassing importance. Then their 'competence', so to speak, is taken to exceed its proper bounds, and the corresponding subsidiarisation or ordering of the knower becomes a personal, even ecstatically personal, commitment to a sub-personal object, and is thus an agony – a contention between a personal commitment and a sub-personal 'object' of commitment.

Of course, the 'proper bounds' of such aspects or ideas of another human being are only apparent in a higher focal awareness of the other. How is that achieved? One way is to 'back into' it by discovering the mistakenness of taking lesser focal awareness beyond their level of competence. That is the possibility obliquely indicated by the so-called 'Peter Principle' (after its originator). Citing many case-studies, Dr Peter suggests that 'in a hierarchy every employee tends to rise to his level of incompetence' – his success at one level tends to earn him promotion into another position at a level beyond his competence; but the mistake is only discovered after the fact. Focal awareness of the higher level arises when there is evidence that a focal awareness from a lower level has been extended beyond its sphere of competence; the 'old' focal awareness is then subsidiarised by the new, and seen as having proper bounds which it cannot exceed successfully. The other is then seen in his proper competence, and this brings an appropriate ordering of relationships for those who know him. But all this happens by backing out of a focal awareness which has become problematic.

In the example just discussed there is another problem – whether the *frame of reference* is appropriate. It dealt with *competence*, and suggested that appropriate relationships would be ordered (subsidiarised) when a suitable focal awareness was achieved in these terms; a human being focally seen as competent within certain limits would bring about the ordering (subsidiarising) of the one who knew him, and their relationship, in terms of competences and achievements. A client seen by a social worker as a problem, that is 'focussed' in terms of competence, would subsidiarise the social worker and their mode of relationship in terms of competence also – evoking the social worker's competence in sorting out problems and eliciting the information needed in order to do so. Such a social worker might not be able to see the client in any other terms.

So achieving a high focal awareness of another human being may be a matter not only of finding the mistakenness of taking lesser focal awareness beyond their level of appropriateness but also of finding the limitations of certain frames of reference. And the history of human understanding provides a long list of such frames of reference – which can only provide terms for sub-personal focal awareness: all the attempts to find design and pattern in and beyond the world in terms of sub-human rational patterns, those which see this pattern in terms of substance, structure, idealised numbers, machines, organic regularities, measurable achievements, and so on. Given the convincing manner in which these frames of reference are used, it is actually very difficult to find their limitations – to 'back into' a higher frame of reference by 'backing out' of them. The problem is to find the limits, not simply of an *employee's* competence, but of *thinking* of human beings in terms of *competence* or achievement.

The other way of achieving a higher focal awareness of another is to 'grasp' it positively – as opposed to establishing its *possibility nega-tively*. This positive approach to a higher focal awareness is not a 'grasping' in the sense that the focal awareness can be *produced* by striving after it, but it is a *believing* in a *framework* which makes a higher focal awareness *possible*. Hence, as Polanyi says, we must 'recognize belief . . . as the source of all knowledge'; 'no intelligence, however critical and original, can operate outside such a fiduciary framework'.[7] Our convictions or 'system of acceptances' incorporate us into a frame-work of fundamental beliefs which have their own basic premises, and 'which are validated by becoming happy dwelling-places of the human mind'.[8]

A positive approach to a higher focal awareness is *made possible* by an accepted and in-dwelt framework. Such a framework needs to become so 'natural' – despite the feelings of inadequacy one may have – that it allows the focal awareness to emerge. It also needs to become so reasonable that it can stand against alternatives which may present themselves. Only thus can it become a matter of 'passionate impulse'. Here we see the fashion in which a framework, indwelt and supported by evidence, itself commands personal commitment. But it is essential to recognise that the main justification of the framework, and personal commitment to it, is what it *makes possible* in focal awareness and its correlative subsidiarisation. The framework and belief in it *are not* the focal awareness and its reordering of the 'knower'; they make such things possible.

But if such a positive approach is possible in achieving a higher focal awareness of another what kind of frame of reference will bring fully human subsidiarisation? Certainly, Polanyi is correct in stressing the intellectual beauty of personal vision and personal initiative as essential factors in good scientific work; 'the distinctive ability of a scientific discoverer lies in the capacity to embark successfully on lines of enquiry which other minds, faced with the same opportunities, would not have recognised or not have thought profitable'.[9] And he is also right in emphasising that the scientist's allegiance to universal intellectual standards happens by the scientist's personal acknowledgment of their jurisdiction over him. Still again, he is correct in showing that, by contrast with these personal matters, *subjectivity* results when the individual *disengages* himself from this *personal* vision, initiative and acknowledgment, in effect making them impersonal through seceding from them and making them objects to be reflected upon. But these considerations, while important guidelines, do not give more than a preliminary indication of the kind of frame of reference we need. The question is: how do we construe the other and be ourselves – fully?

One important aspect of the answer is to say that we do not. As Polanyi says of St. Augustine's maxim 'unless you believe, you shall not understand', 'it says that the process of examining any topic is both an exploration of the topic, and an exegesis of our fundamental beliefs in the light of which we approach it. . . . Our fundamental beliefs are continuously reconsidered in the course of such a process, but only within the scope of their own premisses'.[10] So any focal awareness of another demands continuous readjustment of the fundamental frame within which we see it, and as we have seen demands continuous resubsidiarisation of our behaviour toward it. This is much like the continuous alteration of the 'ground' as the 'figure' alters in music or in painting: in music, the changing melodic foreground demands a ground which changes in a changing complementary relationship to the melody.

And there is no reason to suppose that there is an end to this process of change. It should be directed toward a more adequate focal awareness of the other, and the continuous reconsideration should therefore *ascend*, bringing a more adequate 'frame'. But this is desired in order to *respect* the other, to know the other *as other*. This 'barrier', which constitutes the 'privacy' of the other, also is part of the knower's fundamental respect for the other; it is a forbidding to the knower of the hidden depths of what he seeks to know, and at the same time a self-denying by the knower which prevents him from probing too deeply – the other is not to be *possessed* in knowledge or in any other

86

way. The distance has to be maintained, for the sake of known and knower. So when I seek to befriend another, I must in knowing, not seek to end our difference.

What is implicit in this is an *affirmation* of the other as an 'unreachable height'. Polanyi speaks of 'reconsidering beliefs but only within the scope of their own premisses', and we must recognise that considering the other as an 'unreachable height' is a premiss, one which disqualifies any approach as fully adequate. Likewise it disqualifies attempts to possess or intervene in the free activity of the other.

But the affirmation is not only denial and disqualification – it is also the means by which the knower comes 'within range of hearing' of the other. It is the means by which the other is given the possibility of expressing its own splendour. At one and the same time, two things happen: the other comes to expression *and* expressive language is instituted by which the other is known. In other words, when the other is affirmed, the knower is no longer giving himself what is to be known, he and their relationship are constituted by the other.

What is being affirmed though? To consider the other as an unreachable height which expresses its own splendour is an ideal for aesthetic recognition, but not yet sufficient either for a focal awareness of another human being or for a fully human subsidiarisation. As an example of what can go wrong, consider Hannah Tillich's account of her husband's behaviour at a party shortly after their marriage:

'He had left me often, flirting with other women, leaving each one in turn for another at the succeeding dinner party. I had to take care of the spurned one, who came to me shamelessly complaining about Paulus's faithlessness, which amused me'.[11]

Tillich's fascination with each woman was an affirmation, but only occasional and short-lived, in which each was 'left in turn' – apparently because of the hidden premiss that the excitingly hidden and the new were intrinsically better. Ironically, his wife is the constant one, at least in this episode, constant in caring for the cast-offs. But as their lives showed, neither could be said to have developed fully personal relationships. And Tillich's *theology* reflects this occasionalism, lacking any element of loyal perseverance. The lack of an adequate focal awareness of God was matched by an inadequate subsidiarisation of personal behaviour and relationship with God. On the one hand, God seen as an ultimately unspecifiable ground of being is a sub-personal constancy; and on the other hand, the activity of life and faith ('accepting that you are accepted') bespeaks an off-and-on activity in which constancy and loyalty are never achieved.

So considering the other as an unreachable height, and respecting or affirming the other as such, is also allowing one's relationship to the other to be constituted by the other and brought to expression in a 'new' language. But all these require patience and endurance, not as one's achievements or competence, but because the affirmation intrinsic to one's focal awareness of the other brings these characteristics of the subsidiarisation which occurs and 'patterns' one's awareness and behaviour.

Suppose a black person, acutely aware of himself as black because of years of rejection and deprivation as 'blackie', faces a white person not so aware of himself as white because he has never been rejected or deprived because of his colour (though he may have been in other ways). Each, of course, may 'rationalise' the other in various kinds of focal awareness, and behave or relate to him accordingly. 'You are a white racist whether you know it or not: that's your problem which you'll have to sort out − I won't be a "token" black for you'. 'But you are too much aware of your blackness, and you'll have to overcome that yourself: I haven't created − nor can I change − the system which has oppressed you'. In such a situation the basis of identity and behaviour for each is in his focal awareness of the other. This focal awareness is in stereotypes, however, static images which confine and hold the other still and at a distance; the distance is not born of respect and affirmation for the other as he is, nor does it generate new language or patient endurance − it is a distance of disregard or detachment at least, or of enmity and manipulation at worst, and correspondingly deadens relationship and language.

Between these two, there can be another kind of affirmation and respect, arising with another focal awareness, when what had been 'your problem' becomes 'my problem' as well, when the other is 'seen as a human being', treated as such, and is accorded 'the right to develop as a normal human being'. This is the moment when the 'unreachable height' of the other is affirmed, and disregard and manipulation cease; but it is also the moment when a new communication is constituted between the two − a new relationship of trust, hope and mutual commitment.

So the unreachable height of the other is only 'one side' of the premiss operative within focal awareness of another human being. The 'other side' is new relationship and new communication and new commitment. The affirmation of the other as *unreachable* and yet *present* occurs as an active use of this premiss without which there could be no such focal awareness as we have been indicating.

What is the nature of this premiss? Normal usage suggests that 'regulative presuppositions' for focal awareness are inert ideas or fixed principles. But it is evident that fixities have their usefulness only when one is focally aware of the regular and fixable – cobblestones – and that their usability decreases progressively as one goes beyond, to problems and people. At these higher levels, premisses acquire a different character, and provide a dynamic order, a freedom in which one lives, an economy of life. In other words, they are indwelt as a basis for awareness and behaviour, and this becomes the ground for focal awareness and the consequent subsidiarisation. So, when black man meets white man, they are held together by the dynamic order in each (as premiss) which brings each to be aware of the other's aspirations and problems (as focal awareness) and thereby reordered in thought and behaviour as 'for him' (as subsidiarisation). This, of course, is what allows and enables Christians to see another aright, 'put heart into him' and to 'assure him of (their) love by a formal act'. (II Cor. 2.7-9)

What is the provenance of this premiss, though? What constitutes this dynamic order as possible for a human being, or for two of them together? Perhaps it happens because it is *made* possible by *them*, perhaps during the course of a long struggle: that is the suggestion of humanists, whether existentialist, atheist or Buddhist. But his view not only *dulls* human possibilities to what human beings can manage, it is also at odds with the whole structure of affirmation which we have been considering, which suggests that our 'order' arises from a focal awareness of the other. Following that line of argument brings us to conclude that the premiss necessary for being aware of the person of another is a dynamic ordering in us and that that premiss arises in our affirmation of the personal dynamic ordering of God. In other words, the premiss arises in our allegiance to, or our worship of, God – God who is 'premissed' thereby as One whose own being is a personal dynamic. Polanyi is correct in emphasising that fundamental religious premisses (e.g. 'God exists') arise in worship, but perhaps not fully enough aware of *what* arises there.[12] What, or rather *who*, arises there is a dynamic and personal ordering which alone brings the possibility of fully personal awareness and relationship.

The *content* of the 'premiss' which arises in worship is no abstract personal principle, not even one which is symbolically concrete in the world, but the life of the Trinity made present in the life, sufferings, death and resurrection of Jesus. That is what sustains us in fully personal focal awareness and the relationship which follows from it.

NOTES TO CHAPTER 4

1. Anthony Storr, *The Integrity of the Personality*, 1963, p. 22
2. Yehudi Menuhin, *Unfinished Journey*, London, 1978, p. 189
3. *Ibid.*, p. 187
4. Michael Polanyi, 'Problem-Solving' in *The British Journal for the Philosophy of Science*, Vol. VIII, 1957, p. 92
5. Robert Pirsig, *Zen and the Art of Motorcycle Maintenance*, London, 1975, p. 34
6. Michael Polanyi, *Duke Lectures*, microfilmed at Pacific School of Religion, 1964, quoted in Marjorie Grene, *The Knower and the Known*, London, 1966, p. 219.
7. Michael Polanyi, *Personal Knowledge*, p. 266f
8. *Ibid.*, p. 280
9. *Ibid.*, p. 301
10. *Ibid.*, p. 267
11. Hannah Tillich, *From Time to Time*, 1974, p. 145
12. Michael Polanyi, *Personal Knowledge*, p. 279f

5

THE TRUTH OF CHRISTOLOGY

COLIN E. GUNTON

It is not too much of a simplification to say that the great dividing line in modern theology is drawn by that watershed in Western thought known as the Enlightenment. The attitude of the theologian to this aspect of his past does much to determine how he will regard the classical documents of the Christian faith, in particular the Bible and the theology of the Fathers and Councils. The most extreme proponents of an 'enlightened' theology will be tempted to take rather a patronising stance in relation to that classical past: what in a similar context Dr Stephen Prickett has called a mixture of scepticism and naivety, straining at gnats and swallowing camels. It is almost as if modern man is to be seen as a different species, decisively superior to those minds that produced all thought before the Renaissance.

Of course, that is a parody and a caricature, unfair but with elements of truth. And the chief element of truth is to be found in the attitudes engendered in that Copernican revolution described by Karl Barth in the opening chapters of his *Protestant Theology in the Nineteenth Century*, the transformation of an earth-centred view of the universe into a man-centred one. The age of absolutism, as he called it, made all to centre on man, who eventually ran the risk of putting himself where Feuerbach wanted him, in the place of God himself, with all the destructive consequences our world is now experiencing. In the intellectual sphere, the consequence is of a certain conception of reason: functioning as autonomously standing in judgment upon its objects. Michael Polanyi's great significance here lies in providing one of the ways into a critique of man-centred rationalism. But how justifiable is it to attempt to relate the thought of a philosopher of science and of society to a relatively specialised area of human reflection, that concerning the doctrine of the Person of Christ? Little that

Polanyi has written refers directly to the kind of problems with which Christology appears to be concerned. Any interpreter must therefore tread gingerly. There is an advantage, for the very lack of direct treatment of this topic in Polanyi's work gives him freedom to range widely within his subject's writings. But that advantage is balanced by an equivalent danger, that ideas wrenched from their context will be forcibly applied to a topic to which they are only vaguely relevant.

Accordingly, the method of approach will be as follows. It will be recognised that two distinct subjects are under review. Their relation will therefore be seen as one of exploratory conversation rather than of a too hasty joining in marriage. Or perhaps the relation can be understood with the aid of one of Polanyi's own central teachings. It is that concerning the function of tacit knowledge. Human knowing always involves attending through something which is tacitly known to an object which can be explicitly known only by means of the already existing tacit knowledge, as when the meaning of a sentence is understood by attending through the words in which, as they are employed as tools, so to speak, the meaning is expressed. Once turn the attention directly to the individual words, or to the sound of those words independently of their meaning, and the whole that is intended by the sentence is lost.[1] If we are not in like manner to lose track of our discussion, attention must first be given to central problems of modern Christological thought. These can only be discussed with the assistance of a wide range of tacit accomplishments: inherited concepts and the result of historical debates among them. But they will also be approached here with one that has been acquired especially for the occasion. What do the problems of Christology look like when seen through the instrumentality of a mind that has immersed itself in the philosophy of Polanyi, his commentators and his critics?

Dualism

There are two overwhelmingly apparent features of contemporary Anglo-Saxon, and especially English, Christology: its subjectivism and historicism. The latter is defined by Polanyi as the method of 'striving to judge past events by the standards of their own time', a method which, 'when taken to its limit . . . fosters an extreme, altogether fallacious, relativism'.[2] The former reveals itself in a tendency to deny that there can be any Christology at all, in the sense of a doctrine asserting certain propositions about Jesus, and claiming them to be true objectively, independent of the believer or the community of belief. Leaving the question of historicism on one side for the moment, we shall first follow up the theme of subjectivism.

The roots of this tendency in Western Christology lie far back in our history, probably as far back as Augustine. But the decisive development took place in the nineteenth century, and is well introduced by a brief look at the use made by continental theologians of a much quoted saying from a theologian of the Reformation. 'To know Christ', said Melanchthon, 'is to know his benefits'. This can be taken to imply, and was certainly later made to imply, that to know Christ is to know *no more than* his benefits. In other words, there is no knowledge of Christ other than that of his benefits, or, crudely, than what is mediated by his effects upon me. If effects are all that matter, what need is there for a Christology which is claimed to be true independently of the human experience of this or that individual? There can be little doubt that a radicalising of Melanchthon's dictum must lead to thorough subjectivism, though that is not to say that it is always so construed.

A useful example for our purposes is to be found in the work of Albrecht Ritschl, whose thought-forms are to be found repeated in so much modern Christology. He too appealed to Melanchthon, and argued: 'If Christ by what he has done and suffered for my salvation is my Lord, and if, by trusting for my salvation to the power of what he has done for me I honour him as my God, then that is a value-judgment of a direct kind. It is not a judgment which belongs to the sphere of disinterested scientific knowledge like the formula of Chalcedon'.[3] Ritschl's famous appeal to value-judgment and its contra-distinction from scientific knowledge – a very Kantian distinction, of course – has the effect of shifting the onus of Christological statement from the object of faith to the believer. The final sentence contains a world of meaning: theological judgment does not belong to 'disinterested scientific knowledge like the formula of Chalcedon'.[3]

Now, the formula of Chalcedon represents a summary and perfecting of the Church's belief in Christ as it had developed up to the middle of the fifth century after Christ. It certainly does not totally neglect the side of the subject: 'Wherefore, following the holy Fathers, we all with one voice confess our Lord Jesus Christ . . .' are its opening words. But it is more interested in the object of belief: who and what Jesus Christ *is*. It is for this reason that most of the original and creative Protestant theologians of the nineteenth century rejected the definition as the outcome of an impossible ideal, or at best only secondary to what was really central and important. But secondary to what?

The answer to that question is to be found in the massive achievement of 'the father of modern theology', and particularly in the famous 'Introduction' to *The Christian Faith*. Dogmatic statements, says Schleiermacher, must be primarily descriptions of the inner experience or religious consciousness of the believer. Two other types of proposition are possible: 'utterances regarding the constitution of the world may belong to natural science, and conceptions of divine modes of action may be purely metaphysical . . .' But insofar as they contain any theological content propositions must be developed out of the descriptions of the religious consciousness. Schleiermacher is not saying that such scientific and metaphysical statements are necessarily false or irrelevant, but that they are if taken on their own, for 'both are engendered on the soil of science, and so belong to the objective consciousness and its conditions, and are independent of the inner experience and the facts of the higher self-consciousness'.[4]

I am not concerned here to decide whether, in the context of eighteenth- and nineteenth-century scientific rationalism, Schleiermacher's was the right direction to take. But two things seem to me to be crucial and almost beyond dispute. First, whatever its intention, the outcome of the trend begun by Schleiermacher has been the radical subjectivising of the Christian faith. From saying that a thing is secondary to dismissing it as irrelevant is a smaller step than the one which Schleiermacher originally took of transferring from object to subject the primary reference of theological assertion. And the step has been taken, as is evident from the title of one of Maurice Wiles' influential articles, 'Was Christology based on a Mistake?' a question manifestly expecting and inviting the answer 'Yes'. If theology is primarily concerned with formulating statements about the subject of belief, may it not be that the secondary statements about its object come to be seen as in some way running counter to or falsifying the statements about the subject, expecially in an age when traditional doctrines have supposedly been subject to criticisms from which they will never recover? If the secondary runs counter to the primary, it is no longer secondary, but false and must be discarded. Thus it is that a recent article in support of Schleiermacher's theological method wonders whether the great theologian might himself have been better advised to push through his concentration on the religious consciousness to its limits –

that is to say, to do for himself what others have since done for him, and to dispense altogether with the objective metaphysical content he illegitimately gave to his concept of God.[5]

The second important aspect of Schleiermacher's revolution is that it introduced into theology a radical distinction between the methodology of theology and that of other disciplines, especially the natural sciences. The one is seen to belong primarily to the sphere of the subject, the other to that of the object. Theology has to do with things of the subject, science with things whose truth is to be judged in abstraction from any relation to the subject. The scientific and the religious spheres are different worlds, and to be approached by entirely different routes.

Now, it is conceivable that such an approach might save theology from destruction in an age dominated by the success of the natural sciences. But it can only be a temporary reprieve for, on this understanding, it becomes impossible to formulate a public or interpersonal criterion of truth in theology. Not only does every man quite properly believe what is true in his own eyes, but there is no intersubjective way by which he may test and assess the truthfulness of his beliefs. The concept of truth becomes vacuous and redundant, and thus the dualism of subject and object, of theology and science, ultimately destructive of theology.

Objectivism

Suppose, however, that Schleiermacher correctly diagnosed the problem. Theology has to be done in a culture dominated by the methods, presuppositions and successes of the natural sciences. Among these presuppositions are those theories elaborated by the great names of modern philosophy. Let us briefly notice two of them. First there is Descartes, whose thought is dominated by his quest for certainty, for utterly indubitable truths. The locus of the certainty he claims to find is himself, and particularly the realm of his ideas. If an idea can be clearly and distinctly conceived, then it is true. Polanyi would see in this a quest for the impossible: for explicit, exhaustive knowledge which, because of its ideal content, is totally independent of the one who knows it. Its outcome is a dualism between knower and known which cannot be resolved because subject and object are made absolute and opposed to each other by the nature of their essential characteristics.

Second there is Immanuel Kant who, conscious of the irresolvable difficulties presented both by Descartes and the British empiricists, attempted to redraw the boundaries between subject and object. His method was to shift the balance to the side of the subject. What we call the material world is known only because the human mind imposes upon it a conceptual structure through which it is known: we see the world according to certain patterns, of which causality and substance are perhaps the most important, and we do so because the mind is, in Bertrand Russell's famous illustration, like a pair of coloured spectacles imposing their pattern upon the presented manifoldness of our perceptual experience. But, paradoxically, this does not make the view of knowledge any less objectivist. Quite the reverse. The spectacles are those provided for Kant by none other than Isaac Newton, whom Kant much revered. They cause us to see the world as mechanistic, and therefore the outcome is in no way essentially different from Descartes' in the absolute division between knower and known. It was against a Kantian background in particular that both Schleiermacher and Ritschl operated, and it forced them into making their division, which is parallel to Kant's own division between pure and practical reason, between the objective knowledge of science and the subjective world of the religious believer.

The whole thrust of Polanyi's epistemology is directed against rigid dichotomies of this kind. His is not an imperialist theory, however, attempting to impose a uniform criterion of knowledge, as always seems to be the danger of Lonergan's post-Kantian Thomism. It is rather to show that all areas of human knowing share the same kind of structure, whatever differences appropriate to the various objects of knowledge must also be allowed. This latter stress upon the differences within the world of human knowledge emerges most clearly in some of the developments revealed in Polanyi's final work, *Meaning*, edited in book form by Harry Prosch, and should not be forgotten. But our chief interest here is in the primary, unitive, epistemology.

The first thing to say is that for Polanyi *all* human knowledge is personal in the sense that it is only achievable *by a person*. This is not the same as saying that it is subjective, but it is certainly different from the ideals of scientific objectivism set out in the quotations from Schleiermacher and Ritschl. Only persons are able to know, because knowledge involves the use of, and therefore depends upon, what Polanyi has called our tacit powers. Of course, the possession of tacit powers is not restricted to persons: rats, for example, display them in solving problems concerning their food supply. But human explicit knowing can be shown to involve the development of the powers present in such lower levels of living reality at a higher, articulate, level. Not only does articulate knowledge involve the use of tacit powers, of learning and of language, as instruments; but, more important for our purposes, elements of those tacit powers are not patient of fully explicit articulation. This is illustrated both by Polanyi's use of the Gödelian doctrines of the impossibility of the exhaustive formalisation of theories[6] and by his contention that higher levels of scientific understanding become *increasingly* dependent upon a personal and tacit component: 'The meaning of experimental embryology is . . . doubly dependent on personal knowlege: both in respect of the unspecifiable knowledge of true shapes, and in respect of the appreciation of the process by which highly significant shapes and structures are brought into existence'.[7] The outcome is that the highest flights of scientific achievement are furthest from the ideals of scientific knowledge propounded by Descartes and assumed so unquestioningly by Schleiermacher and Ritschl. There is no knowledge which is not subjective, when subjective means *requiring a subject*.

But this is not to say that it is subjective in any sense entailing subjectivism or relativism. As Professor Torrance has shown, the opposite is true: 'personal knowledge . . . has nothing to do with the inclusion of a personal, far less a subjective, factor in the content of knowledge, for the personal participation on the part of the scientist relates to the bearing of all his thought and statement upon objective reality, insofar as it is accessible to human understanding and description'.[8] This objective aspect of Polanyi's theory will concern us more fully in the next section. Here it is mentioned to prevent misunderstanding of this attempt to show that, if Polanyi is right, scientific knowledge is not what many theologians have thought it to be, and that therefore one side of the distinction between scientific (objective) and theological (subjective) knowledge disappears. This in turn requires that the other pole of the dichotomy be examined, for the two stand together as the joint implicates of a post-Kantian philosophy. If scientific knowledge is not objectivistic according to the received tradition, perhaps a like critique may be applied to the subjectivising of faith and theology.

Subjectivism

To begin with, it must be made clear that this is not a plea for a bare objectivism in theology. There *is* a sense in which 'to know

Christ is to know his benefits'. Even the austerely objective Calvin affirms that 'the mere name of God attributed to Christ will affect us little, if our faith do not feel it to be such by experience'.[9] But to speak of the existential implications of a belief is a far different thing from reducing the faith to nothing but the impact upon the subject of something otherwise unknown and unknowable. Polanyi's theory of personal knowledge also makes possible a critique of the idea of purely or primarily subjective knowledge. The reason is this: there *is* no knowledge simply of the contents of the mind, because that content cannot be understood in abstraction from the world from which it derives. (This could be taken in a Kantian sense, but is not so meant, as should become clear). The best introduction to this topic is provided by Polanyi's theory of indwelling.

Just as the theory of personal knowledge results from the generalisation of a theory of perception to cover all types of knowledge, so this theory represents the generalisation of a metaphor taken from the human usage of tools as extensions of the body. When a blind man uses a stick, or someone uses a probe to explore a hidden cavity, he learns about the world by their instrumentality, *from* them *to* the object of knowledge. Employing these tools tacitly, we *indwell* them, 'this indwelling being logically similar to the way we live in our body. . . . (Indwelling) applies here in a logical sense as affirming that the parts of the external world, when interiorised, function in the same way as our body functions when we attend from it to things outside'.[10] It is important to note here that for Polanyi indwelling is a '*logical*' relationship, 'that links life in our body to our knowledge of things outside. . . .' It is the fact that there is a real relation, in which there is a rational linkage between mind and matter, that makes the generalisation from body to tool to sophisticated theory a possibility: 'when we attend from a set of particulars to the whole which they form, we establish a logical relation between the particulars and the whole, similar to that which exists between our body and the things outside it'.[11] The way in which our bodies and by extension our tools, both physical and theoretical, make a real indwelling in the world possible is fundamental to Polanyi's case. Without it, there would be no knowledge of the world at all. Thus the theory of indwelling is the obverse of the theory of tacit knowing. The latter demonstrates the irreducibly personal nature of knowing; the former its irreducible orientation to the real world. This suggests that it is a mistake to reduce perception, as Hume attempted to reduce it, to the impact upon us of some unknown and unknowable object. At least in our knowledge of the physical world there is shown to be an interrelation of subject and object which maintains the distinction between the two without making either absolute. The world can be known because we indwell some parts of it as a means to knowing other parts. Indwelling presupposes a real relation of mind and body, person and world, concept and reality, and is illustrated at its highest level by the relation between mathematical theory and the universe.[12]

It does not follow automatically that these considerations can be held to apply also in the sphere of the knowledge of God in Jesus Christ. But Polanyi does give us good reason to believe that the theories of knowledge on which subjectivist Christologies are so heavily dependent are false. In particular they do not have the right to claim that they represent the only possible view of modern scientific epistemology. What the argument so far, therefore, serves to suggest is that it is a mistake to confuse a Christology which has existential relevance with one which is concerned solely with the associated subjective experience. The liberal tradition in Christology is wrong to suggest that theological knowing must of necessity be of an entirely different kind from that of modern scientific thought, for both its characterisation of objective scientific knowledge and its attempt to mark out a distinctive field for the exercise of religious understanding mistake the very nature of human knowing. It fails to see, in particular, that knowledge involves the interaction of subject and object, or better, of the person and his world, in which the one has a real relation to the other, which articulate knowledge then, in its turn, more or less successfully reflects. It is this genuine interaction of mind and reality that is the key to it all. We are by it not banned from any use of the subject-object distinction, but rather freed from, in Helmut Kuhn's words, 'regarding this relationship as the axis around which the philosophical cosmos has to turn'.[13] In other words, we do not have an absolute dualism which forces us to choose between a totally objective and therefore abstract set of theological doctrines and a subjectivism in which all revolves around the ego of the individual believer. Because a knowledge in which subject and object are in real interaction obtains in other areas, we may proceed on the hypothesis that it is conceivable in this case, too. Thus if the argument so far is correct, we can claim to have established the necessary though not the sufficient conditions for claiming that theological doctrines like those concerning the Person of Christ may properly be held to be true.

We now arrive directly at the second of the problems outlined at the beginning of this paper, that of historicism. If we are to assert the truth of a traditional Christology – i.e. one which holds that in Jesus Christ, who is both fully God and fully man, God has entered our time and history in order to reconcile mankind to himself – then we must also be able to claim some kind of knowledge of historical events whose meaning cannot be limited to their temporal context alone. There are those who claim the contrary, that historical events may only be understood by analogy with events known to us now, and that therefore it is impossible to hold to the meaningful uniqueness of one particular past event or groups of events. Does Polanyi help us here?

An entry to the problem is provided by Helmut Kuhn, in his discussion of the question of historicism and the relativism which so often accompanies it. He begins by calling attention to the parallels between the philosophy of history of Dilthey and his school and Polanyi's theory of personal knowledge. 'Like Polanyi, the German followers of Dilthey . . . emphatically reject an "objectivist" conception of knowledge. . . . The one who understands has to place himself, by an act of imaginative empathy, in the centre of the experiential context. . . . The knowledge resulting from this act may well be described as an "indwelling" . . .'[14] Yet there are also important differences between the two, 'a skeleton at the banquet of the philosophers feasting on historical erudition and indulging in dreams of humanistic grandeur. . . . The name of the unbidden guest was relativism.'[15] This relativism derived from a demythologisation of Hegel's philosophy of history. Bereft of Hegel's faith in the rationality of history, Hegel's formula about philosophy as 'its time comprehended in thoughts' now 'simply expresses a surrender to relativism. But accepting relativism actually means to relinquish the idea of philosophy'[16] – and, we might add, of Christology, for that, *a fortiori*, is bound up with judgments about the meaning of the past. The outcome is that an apparent alliance with Polanyi ends up in the very position he is concerned to attack: 'knowledge is personal knowledge indeed, but in a sense which obliterates the distinction between personal and subjective. . . . Knowledge is either personal, relevant and untrue, or impersonal, irrelevant and true'.[17] It is not surprising, concludes Kuhn, that Dilthey's successors Heidegger and Sartre fell prey to political ideologies of right and left.[18]

Kuhn's analysis seems to me to be both penetrating and useful. His own argument bears primarily on philosophy, and holds that Polanyi's conception of personal knowledge, with its correlative return to a hierarchically-conceived cosmology, makes possible the restoration of philosophy in its classical form; for once again, we might add, Polanyi has revealed a real interrelation of knowing and being. Our problems with Christology are somewhat different, for the conception of the reality of God's historical interaction with the world is not of itself guaranteed by the idea of layered reality, though it may be facilitated by it. It is facilitated by the general point, expressed by Professor T. F. Torrance, that Polanyi's theories of knowing and being 'manifest a universe with an in-built principle of transcendence and a framework of knowing in which the human mind is left open at its own boundary conditions to the intimations and the indeterminate implications of reality transcending it altogether'.[19] But a cosmologically conceived transcendence does not in itself make possible an understanding of the interrelationship of God and the world mediated through particular historical events. Indeed, long ago the combination of a cosmologically conceived transcendence and a hierarchically stratified universe led to the phenomenon known as Arianism. We shall therefore have to move beyond Helmut Kuhn's argument if we are to enable Polanyi's insights to bear directly upon questions of Christology. But the end of Kuhn's paper does offer a promising avenue of exploration. Among Dilthey's successors, he says, it is H.-G. Gadamer who 'makes an energetic effort toward overcoming relativism by rendering to historical interpretation its objective dignity'.[20] Perhaps rightly, Kuhn seems to be sceptical of Gadamer's success. But, nonetheless, a glance at some of the themes of *Truth and Method* will take us a little further along our way.

Gadamer shares with Polanyi a concern to break out of the strait-jacket of the Enlightenment's conception of rationality. His critique of that era's 'prejudice against prejudice' has parallel features with Polanyi's doctrine of the fiduciary aspects of knowledge, while, like the latter, he shows a desire to expunge the rigid line of demarcation between the natural and human sciences. What is interesting for us is his theory of the interpretation of texts, for Christology is essentially bound up with a divine history that is mediated through documents recording at once a history and its significance. Gadamer rejects any theory of indwelling that claims or entails 'the superiority of the interpreter over his object'.[21] Rather, he holds, it is the task of the interpreter to let the text take possession of his mind. Interpretation of an authoritative text then becomes a kind of conversation within a living tradition between a reader and the text that stands objectively over against him. There is a real interaction of subject and object, not unlike that discerned by Polanyi in the practice of both everyday human perception and specialised scientific discovery. Just as for Polanyi human discovery is made possible as reality discloses its hidden depths to us, so human interpretation eventuates when a text, far from being lost in cultural relativism, by the power of its content transcends the temporal gap between itself and us. The point is this. Modern relativism finds itself unable to draw a distinction between the meaning of something and its meaning *for me*, largely because it holds that meaning can only be understood in terms of meaning *for me*. This entails that there is an unbridgeable logical gap between what the New Testament documents mean for me and what they meant to those who wrote them. The latter is unknowable, and therefore any contemporary meaning of a text is reduced to its subjective impact, one more instance of the process of subjectivising that was observed earlier in this paper. Gadamer's theory of interpretation, by arguing for the objective meaning of a text over against its interpreter, fills in one of the gaps left by Polanyi's theory of meaning, of which more in a moment. But there is also a way in which it, in its turn, requires complementary assistance from Polanyi, for it fails in one crucial respect. Gadamer's weakness consists in the fact that he continues to be bound by the post-Kantian doctrine that intelligibility depends upon language.

Over against this let us set Polanyi's view of the emergence of linguistic meaning from lower levels of meaning. The existence of tacit powers in animals reveals that their learning activities, such as they are, represent a response to the *meaning* of their world. The astonishing advance in human achievement is made possible by the emergence of an articulate framework of understanding based upon and therefore not in principle different from the tacit powers of lower orders of being. Thus language is not the sole but rather the supreme vehicle of meaning, meaning which is logically prior to the language in which it is expressed.

What is the significance of all this? In the first place, the study of history can take its place in the panorama of the sciences by means of an extension of the theory of indwelling that avoids the distorting influence so feared by Gadamer. This is spelled out by Polanyi in such works as *The Study of Man.* There the distinctiveness of history is seen in its encompassing the factual uniqueness of human activity in distinction from the theoretical repetitiveness of the physical world, but not in such a way as to constitute a difference in principle. Rather, there is a scale of sciences from mathematical physics to the study of history.[22] He sums up:

> 'Every pebble is unique, but profoundly unique objects are
> rare. Wherever these are found (whether in nature or among
> the members of human society) they are interesting in them-
> selves. They offer opportunity for intimate indwelling and for
> a systematic study of their individuality. Since great men are
> more profoundly unique than any object in nature, they sustain
> a far more elaborate study of uniqueness than any natural
> object can. Hence the peculiar position of dramatic history at
> the end of a row of sciences of increasing intimacy and delicate
> complexity, yet offset against all of them by an exceptionally
> vigorous and subtle participation in its subject matter'.[23]

When compared with the sophistication of modern theological engagement with the philosophy of history, Polanyi's remarks might appear crude and fragmentary, and perhaps not untouched by Romantic conceptions of history. They would clearly benefit from the additional insights provided by discussions of hermeneutical theory. But, as over against the theories of historicism, they have the great advantage of showing that the study of man need not be violently severed from the study of nature. Mankind is seen in the context of the whole cosmos, and therefore mankind today need not be cut adrift by accidents of his culture from mankind of other times and places, as post-Enlightenment thought is so often driven to suppose. Further, because of what Polanyi calls human conviviality, the concept of tradition plays a central part in all interpretation, including the sciences. Disciplines like theology which have a large stake in tradition are not ruled out of court *a priori*, and Thomas Langford's appropriation of the notion of indwelling is a justified extension of Polanyi's theory. Speaking of the dogmatic task as it appears in the light of Polanyi's work he says: 'we are related to history not only by indwelling a tradition so that it provides the proximal terms for thought, but also we focus upon (as a distal term) an aspect of that tradition (a specific historical event) and thus find insight not only on the basis of tradition but by re-investigating an aspect of that tradition'.[24] Polanyi, along with Gadamer, enables us to break through the Enlightenment's rejection of tradition by showing that it, too, has a place in all types of scientific enquiry. The texts that come to us from the past do not present a face that is meaningful only to men of their own time, for they can be understood with the aid of all the tacit powers that we and those who came before us have developed in interpersonal and progressive discovery of the depths of meaning there present.

But that only gets us half way, for Christology is not as such the study of history. Historical scepticism and relativism do, as a matter of fact, make it impossible in its traditional sense. But the texts on which traditional Christology has always depended, the books of the New Testament interpreted with the help of the Old, do not purport to be historical records in the sense of Thucydides' *Peloponnesian War* or *The Cambridge Modern History*. They purport to tell a divine-human story, a history that is at once the account of the deeds and sufferings of a man and the reconciling presence of God. To understand their particular and distinctive meaning we must attempt some Polanyian analysis of a Christological text in the light of Polanyi's view of the hierarchical structure of reality.

Chalcedonism

Polanyi's view of hierarchy derives from his analysis of the structure of human knowing. It is expounded with particular clarity in *The Study of Man*, where he shows that the operational principles according to which machines are understood are of a higher level than the physics and chemistry of their component parts, simply because, although the machine depends upon the physics and chemistry for its correct functioning, it cannot be understood *as a machine* in terms of them alone.[25] Analogous to this is the understanding of the operation of an organism: it, too, cannot be understood exhaustively in terms of its physics and chemistry, for the principles of physiology operate at a higher level than those of physics and chemistry, though, once again, the organism is dependent for its correct functioning on those lower levels.[26] But this example leads us to higher levels still, for the analysis of animal behaviour shows that, although dependent upon the proper operation of the organism, it has to be understood, *as behaviour*, at a higher level, for sentient behaviour can be seen to be subject to error, and therefore to presuppose some manner of control by a rational centre.[27] At a higher level still is man, who demands to be understood not only in terms of the capacity for error, but with such notions as respect, value and responsibility. Thus, as we ascend the scale of knowledge we find a corresponding ascent in levels of reality, and are able to conclude that because 'man alone can command respect . . . in this sense we humans are the top of creation'.[28] That is to say, logical and ontological levels are both correlative to each other and classifiable on an ascending scale.

Alongside this let us set parts of a, or rather the, classical text of Christology: 'We all with one voice confess our Lord Jesus Christ one and the same Son, the same perfect in Godhead, the same perfect in manhood, truly God and truly man . . . of one substance with the Father as touching the Godhead, the same of one substance with us as touching the manhood. . . .' These words respond well to Polanyian analysis, for they can be seen to bear many of the marks of a knowledge claim that can be understood in terms of personal knowledge. In particular, they reveal the employment of conceptual tools painfully and carefully developed over several centuries, and become part of the tacit equipment of the Fathers of the Council of Chalcedon. This conceptuality becomes the means through which the writers are viewing the object of their faith as they indwell a tradition of faith and worship that has progressively refined its understanding of its object. This analysis seems to me to be a direct and faithful use of Polanyian terminology, especially in the light of what he has said about the study of history.

And there is yet more that can be said. The text also bears some of the marks of Polanyi's account of how the mind works in making a discovery. No discovery is properly called such unless it takes a logical leap beyond the data it has at hand, being enabled, by its indwelling in the data, to perceive a rational pattern that is really there but has not previously been discerned. Thus might Chalcedon be seen to be an attempt to look *through* the data provided by (i) the New Testament witness to the divine-human interrelation with history, (ii) the worship of the Christian community and (iii) the tradition's rational indwelling in both (i) and (ii), *to* the truth about Jesus Christ. The Dogmatic Formula of Chalcedon is a statement of high scientific precision, condensing into a few sentences that which may be believed about Jesus Christ, and thus presenting in a form that is at once personal and scientific a claim for the truth of Christianity.

But there is also something about the Formula which, because it is unique, does not fit easily into a Polanyian mould. Because obedient and listening response to its single historical revelation has forced its interpreters to see things at two distinct levels, here in a unique union, theological expression is forced to break through all notions of hierarchy. The fundamental distinction between the human and the divine which underlies all that Chalcedon has to say about the one Christ means that here is a reality which, while admitting and indeed demanding the use of human language – for it *is* a fully human, historical reality to which it refers – at once breaks through those categories. The logical levels of Chalcedon do not reflect levels of reality related to each other in a hierarchy. We might almost say that they represent the two levels operating in parallel, though that must not be taken in a Nestorian sense, but only to depict the irreducible duality of the divine-human event, the unique reconciling initiative of God, who has reconciled the irreconcilable in the life and cross and resurrection of his Son. Thus because Christology does reflect and bring to expression the being of God in his becoming for us, it can be held to involve a truth claim. But it claims a truth which is by virtue of its subject-matter, different in some respects from other forms of truth in the manifoldness of human response to the universe.

NOTES TO CHAPTER 5

1. See e.g. *The Study of Man*, p. 30, *Personal Knowledge*, p. 116
2. *The Study of Man*, p. 88. Historicism and its often associated relativism have the effect not only of increasing scepticism about the trustworthiness of the biblical records, but of reinforcing the barrier between ourselves and the historical events that are determinative for faith. They are a typical outcome of 'enlightened' conceptions of reason.
3. Albrecht Ritschl, *The Christian Doctrine of Justification and Reconciliation*, E.T. ed. by H. R. Mackintosh and A. B. Macaulay, 1900, p. 398
4. F. D. E. Schleiermacher, *The Christian Faith*, E.T. ed. by H. R. Mackintosh and J. S. Stewart, 1928, p. 126
5. Van A. Harvey, 'A Word in Defence of Schleiermacher's Theological Method', *Journal of Religion* 42 (1962), pp. 151-70
6. Michael Polanyi, *Personal Knowledge*, pp. 259-61
7. *Personal Knowledge*, p. 357
8. T. F. Torrance, 'The Place of Michael Polanyi in the Modern Philosophy of Science', *Ethics in Science and Medicine*, 1980
9. John Calvin, *Commentary on John* 1.3
10. Michael Polanyi, 'Science and Man's Place in the Universe', in *Science as a Cultural Force*, ed. H. Woolf, 1964, p. 63
11. *Ibid.*, p. 62
12. See e.g. Polanyi's account of the interrelationship between non-Euclidean geometry and relativity theory, *Personal Knowledge*, pp. 8ff and 184ff

13. Helmut Kuhn, 'Personal Knowledge and the Crisis of the Philosophical Tra-
    dition' in *Intellect and Hope. Essays in the Thought of Michael Polanyi*, 1968,
    p. 123
14. *Ibid.*, p. 128
15. *Ibid.*, p. 131
16. *Ibid.*, p. 132
17. *Ibid.*, p. 132
18. *Ibid.*, p. 133
19. T. F. Torrance, *op. cit.*; cf. p. 146f below
20. H. Kuhn, *op. cit.* p. 134
21. Hans-Georg Gadamer, *Truth and Method*, E.T. ed. G. Burden and J. Cumming,
    1975, p. 171
22. Michael Polanyi, *The Study of Man*, p. 83
23. *The Study of Man*, p. 85
24. Thomas A. Langford, 'Michael Polanyi and the Task of Theology', *Journal of
    Religion* 46 (1966), p. 53
25. Michael Polanyi, *The Study of Man*, p. 50f
26. *The Study of Man*, p. 53f
27. *The Study of Man*, p. 58
28. *The Study of Man*, p. 59.

6

PROVIDENCE AND PRAYER

PETER FORSTER

Introduction

Michael Polanyi had a curious relation to religious and theological thought. While he was always prepared to admit the importance of his assertions for the understanding and acceptance of religious belief, he was reluctant to trespass into the field of theology. He was a Christian, but his reasons – as far as he was able to recognise and articulate them – for embracing Christianity rather than any other religion were never made very clear in his writings. Indeed, as he himself tells us, his work was 'not directed toward effecting con-versions to any particular religion',[1] and, as he stated in the last chapter of *Personal Knowledge*, he was not suggesting a 'definite theory concerning the nature of things'.[2] Rather his aim was 'the perhaps more ambitious one to re-equip men with the faculties which centuries of critical thought have taught them to distrust'.[3]

Yet it cannot be denied that Michael Polanyi did desire and envis-age the return of widespread religious belief and practice in our society. Already by 1946 he could end *Science, Faith and Society* by expressing his 'belief that modern man will eventually return to God through the clarification of his cultural and social purposes'.[4] He ends *The Tacit Dimension* (1966) with the hope that the rejection of an absurd vision of the universe 'will open up a meaningful world which could resound to religion'.[5]

I believe that it is one of the tasks of modern theology to take up the challenge and encouragement offered by Polanyi's remarkable achievements. We should sense an opportunity to discover more about the Church's understanding and expression of its message. We should take the risk. I use this word deliberately, for risk it is. It has never been wholly good for the Church to throw its lot in with a particular school of philosophy. Always there has been a tendency for the particular brand of worldly wisdom chosen to become the master rather than the slave of theology's own object and task. We can immediately think of the sterility suffered by theology at the hands of Aristotelian scholasticism, both in Roman Catholic and in Protestant theology, or of the more recent capitulation of theology to Enlightenment humanism. Yet, as even Karl Barth used to say, theology does not fall down from heaven, but is developed and articulated in concepts and language which gain much of their meaning from our understanding of this world and its ways. Of course these concepts and this language must undergo a profound shift in meaning as they are adapted to theology if they are to serve our knowledge of God and his ways. As Michael Polanyi would say, they can only be subsidiary components of our knowledge which is formed by a tacit integration of these subsidiaries. We are here approaching the deep water of a long and arduous theological debate, for it is one of the major objections to any knowledge of God that we cannot argue from the finite and conditioned to God who is infinite and unconditioned. In his own way Michael Polanyi accepted the force of this objection. So theology would seem to find itself committed to the paradox (if we may use this term) of speaking of the unspeakable. This means that while all speech must fail in some degree to express fully the intended meaning of the speaker, our speech is especially imprecise and inadequate when speaking of God. The problem is that we need language to think, but to the extent that we stay at the level of language we get nowhere. Hence, in allowing our language to direct us to God, we need to exercise to a considerable degree our intuition and imagination.

The important point for the present purpose is that the Christian theologian cannot simply start from Michael Polanyi's work and attempt to achieve theological discovery without risking an inevitable departure from knowledge of the living God who reveals himself primarily through his prophets and apostles – the living God of the Bible. Rather, the theologian must start and end with the revelation of this living God, and bring natural or philosophical theology into its exposition as a flexible tool. Polanyi's thought is one such tool – perhaps one of the most useful which are currently available to the theologian.

Let us, then, take two of the central beliefs of Christian theology, the doctrines of providence and prayer, related as they are, and see how Polanyi's thought might help to throw new light upon the traditional doctrines, and vice versa. Why choose providence and prayer? The doctrine of providence has been neglected in our century, when the main areas of theological debate have been elsewhere. It is striking to recall that only 100 or so years ago J. H. Newman could observe a very different state of affairs: 'What Scripture especially illustrates from its first page to its last, is God's Providence; and that is nearly the only doctrine held with a real assent by the mass of religious Englishmen'.[6] The memories of two world wars and their millions of casualties have been too close for many more contemporary theologians and believers to speak affirmatively in this sensitive area of Christian belief and confession, even if we leave aside other more theoretical difficulties which have been recognised. But belief in divine providence is not optional for the Christian, considering the place it occupies in the Bible and the historical development of theology through the centuries. The confession of God as 'Father Almighty' was one of the first and basic components of the creeds of the early Church which we still recite today.

The doctrine of prayer is equally central to the religion of the Bible. Yet it has also been somewhat neglected in recent theology. There have been plenty of Christian leaders and thinkers who have regarded prayer either as a survival from primitive days which should be 'demythologised' and done away with in our modern scientific world, or used as a form of interior reflection and meditation between man and himself, however elaborately it may be dressed up in the 'mythological' robes of a dialogue between man and God. With this latter interpretation room is apparently safeguarded for the practice of prayer as a form of beneficial spiritual exercise. But is this latter conception related to *Christian* prayer, we may well ask? For where is the living God in relation to such activity? The young people of our land, rightly distrustful of hypocrisy, are not impressed by this attempt to keep the form but not the content of Christian prayer. There is a further reason for considering the doctrine of prayer. For what a man believes or does not believe about prayer is a good guide to his religious beliefs in general. What he believes about prayer is an indication of what he believes about God. More particularly, what a man *does* about prayer is an indication of what he believes about it. So, if prayer is prayer *to God*, and the providence of God actually prevails in and over our affairs, it would seem to follow that we ought first to get our ideas straight about God, before we proceed to speak about prayer and providence as such. Or, if this is to attempt to split things inseparable, we should at least be aware that in developing our doctrines (i.e. our articulated understandings) of prayer and providence we inevitably develop, or rely on, an already established doctrine of God. By 'doctrine' I do not of course mean simply the verbal statements of our beliefs. My discussion is offered to the reader's intuition and imagination to direct his or her mind to the meaning of providence and prayer in Christian theology. Throughout I would urge the important and widely applicable maxim: 'Don't listen to what I say, listen to what I mean!'

Finally, a word about my theological axioms, presuppositions, assumptions, beliefs, or whatever. The Old Testament and New Testament traditions have become happy dwelling places for my mind. And I am happy to find that on the whole I am content to stay within the broad lines of Christian tradition as indicated, for example, by the Nicene Creed. But I am no fundamentalist, arguing logically from the individual statements of Scripture, and I am no automatic slave of tradition.

Providence

The Christian believes that God freely resolved in his eternity and richness to create the universe of heaven and earth. In doing this he established a reality distinct from himself, which was neither an extension of his own being nor a reality independently co-existing with him. In this way, the doctrine of creation attempts to avoid a monistic or pantheistic extreme on the one side and a dualistic extreme on the other. Furthermore, on either side simplistic solutions to the problem of the relation or lack of it between God and his creation are also excluded. This creation was thus given its own reality and intelligibility which are different from that of God, but which are in their continuing existence contingent upon God's on-going faithfulness towards his creation. The recognition of this contingency is important. For Christians the world and its history are not ultimately meaningful in themselves, but in relation to God and his purposes. The world is not eternal or explicable in terms of itself. Where Einstein could see the inherent intelligibility of the universe only as a cosmic mystery, the Christian refers to God who is outside and sovereign over the universe.

What was God's purpose as Father, Son and Holy Spirit in creating this universe of heaven and earth? Difficult as it would seem for us humans to answer this question, we can, I think, give the answer that God's purpose was to share his life and love and glory with another reality over which he would be Lord. In other words, God sought to glorify himself in the very action of glorifying his creation which is separate from his own being. In execution of this purpose for his creation, God resolved to interact with the world in a specific way by choosing one nation, Israel, as the representative of all nations, to be his servant. This history culminated in the birth, life, death, resurrection and ascension of God himself who had entered human history as the man Jesus Christ. God's particular purposes in his incarnation can be summarised as twofold. In the first place and fundamentally it was to make atonement and to reconcile the world to himself, because his creation was helplessly afflicted by evil and suffering. God, so the New Testament clearly asserts, came in Jesus to take to himself, the only one who could achieve this, the evil and suffering of his creation. This struggle ended with the cry from the Cross 'It is finished', and God's victory for himself and for his world was announced by Jesus' resurrection from the dead. In the second place, and as a consequence, the event of Jesus Christ creates a new era in world history, the time of the Church, an era which reaches out to the universal declaration of the renewed space and time of God's 'already' achieved redemption of his creation. By renewed space and time I refer to the New Testament hope of a new heaven and new earth. God dwells in the Church (as the 'body' of Christ in time and space) as his primary means of declaring and establishing in the midst of the world afflicted by sin his accomplished redemption, to the final and universal establishment of which creation moves in history.

I have presented a ridiculously compressed outline of traditional Christian belief concerning God's purposes in relation to the world because the characteristic uniqueness in God's relation to the world in his redeeming purposes has been overlooked or played down in the last 250 years. The human mind generally finds difficulty in grasping unique events such as those narrated and witnessed to in the Bible; it prefers to subsume events under general and universal laws. This has been especially true of the mind trained in Western science and humanism. Hence the difficulty in understanding and affirming that only one man was God, the Redeemer of the world. Yet this uniqueness in God's revelation of himself is important in generating the post-Christian moral fervour to which Michael Polanyi has so often referred us.[7] Had no unique Messiah yet come, the thirsting for righteousness, the moral and religious dynamic of the Christian Church, would never have transformed our world in the way that it has. Of course, in the secularisation of the Christian hope, this particularity in God's dealings with us has been transformed into the universal ideologies of the Left and Right which underlie the mass movements of our times, each one claiming a unique and total (i.e. totalitarian) possession of truth.

But that is to digress. I have mentioned all this only to establish that God's general providence for his world is not a general end in itself but occurs for the sake of God's specific purpose. For the Christian the inner meaning of all world history is seen in the life, death and resurrection of Jesus Christ. Conversely, the particular events in the histories of Israel, Jesus, and the Church are the inner meaning of everything that happens in the universe. The Christian can only look to the history narrated in the Bible, which itself leads up to and from the central action of God in the life, death and resurrection of Jesus Christ as the declaration of the truth of God and the truth of man, to see the true meaning of the 'subsidiary particulars'[8] which are constituted by world history generally. He will look from the history of salvation attested in the Bible to the loving God who is active both in the history of salvation and the whole universe. The histories of Israel, Christ, and the Church provisionally anticipate and present to us what will one day be true of all God's creation. This is one way of pointing our minds towards the 'unthinkable consummation',[9] to which we progress.

The central Christian belief here is that all creation serves God's purposes. Everything in creation has its seriousness, its glory or shame, its greatness or littleness — right down to the hairs of our head or the death of a sparrow. How can this be the case? How is creation able to or made to serve God's purposes? Here we reach a question which has proved very problematic in the history of Christian and philosophical thought. The problems have arisen because of the difficulty in maintaining amid their inter-relation both the primacy and reality of God and his will, and the created reality and will of men and creatures and events in creation. It will simplify matters to restrict our present consideration, to some extent at least, to God's providence in relation to human beings. There has been a pronounced tendency, particularly in Western theology, to break up the inter-dependence of Creator and creature and to stress the reality and freedom of one side against the other. In Protestant theology the Calvinist tradition has at times stressed the freedom and will of God to the point of making man into an automaton, and God a rather sinister aristocrat or even tyrant,

while the later Lutheran tradition always tried to safeguard the
dom and will of man as existing independently of the freedom of
This second emphasis may seem preferable, but in its own way
lead to a detachment of the meaning of mankind's existence
God. In Roman Catholic theology the Calvinist position is to
extent mirrored by the Thomists, and the Lutheran by the Jesuits
speak in Polanyian terms, God is neither the totalitarian ruler exe
ing naked power, nor the sceptical relativist.

On each side of the argument there have been unfortunate
ceptions of both God and his creature, man. The God of the
does not create man simply to abandon him to his own activity,
neither does he ignore or overwhelm man's autonomous actuality
activity. Towards his creation, God is neither the apathetic Go
Epicurus, nor the tyrannical God of Stoicism, to relate what
saying to the appropriate schools of ancient philosophy. Rather,
its Lord.[10] Man certainly exercises genuine freedom of choice
therefore self-determination, but in doing so he is not alone b
confronted and accompanied by his Lord. Hence God deter
whether this self-determination of man is good or bad, obedie
disobedient, human or inhuman. The genuine freedom and auton
of man in this regard must be understood comprehensively. The
nothing to be gained from trying to describe the relation betw
God and man by reference only to a restricted part of man's pote
or actually available faculties. This has often enough been tried,
none too impressive results. The unending search for the locus o
imago Dei in man illustrates this. It is the whole man, with his
conscience, emotions, intuitive sense, intellect, tacit dimension
who is free before God. But precisely because he is directly
intimately before the living holy and merciful God, all that he
is done in relation to God who therefore must have a living and a
attitude towards what we do. To adapt a phrase often used by Mic
Polanyi, God sets 'boundary conditions'[11] where there are criteri
which our creaturely activity is judged good or bad, obedient or
obedient. This genuine creaturely freedom of man upon which
insisting is crucial if we are credibly to maintain that God's relatio
man is meaningful for man, that is, if we are to avoid seeing man
sumed and destroyed before the majesty of God.

The aptness of Michael Polanyi's thought in helping us to un
stand and express this situation can be seen in two ways.

Throughout *Personal Knowledge* there recurs the theme of

committing himself in all his knowledge (which is all *personal* knowledge) with universal intent. For Michael Polanyi the idea of a self-centred commitment not involving this bearing on independent and universal reality is subjectivism. Rather, man is always faced with the challenge of reality. Man can do no more than believe as responsibly as possible, with all the attendant risks, and he would evade his calling, and be less than truly human if he aimed his sights lower. For Polanyi, then, it is always reality, i.e. objective reality which exists fundamentally apart from our subjective selves, which decides the measure of truth and falsehood in our belief and action. For the Christian reality is the living God revealed to us in Jesus Christ; Jesus says unambiguously 'I am the truth'.[12] Furthermore, it is in Jesus Christ that we see the perfect man freely obeying God. Here is our standard of true humanity – a humanity conforming to the creating and sustaining will of the Creator and Preserver.

Also presented in *Personal Knowledge*, but more particularly amplified in his later writings, is Michael Polanyi's understanding of the obligation of reality upon man. Reality is not mute, simply awaiting man to make up his mind, but it speaks to man, 'evoking' or 'prompting' (to use Polanyi's own words) a response of commitment. It is this complementary concept of obligation which balances from the objective side the subjective reality of commitment. Here Polanyi recognises an affinity between his views and those of St. Paul: 'The stage on which we thus resume our full intellectual powers is borrowed from the Christian scheme of Fall and Redemption. Fallen man is equated with the historically given and subjective condition of our mind, from which we may be saved by the grace of the Spirit. The technique of our redemption is to lose ourselves in the performance of an obligation which we accept, in spite of its appearing on reflection impossible of achievement. We undertake the task of attaining the universal in spite of our admitted infirmity, which should render the task hopeless, because we trust we will be visited by powers for which we cannot account in terms of our specific capabilities'.[13] To understand Polanyi's achievement here we need to recognise his gradual development of a stratified ontology[14] of the universe which undergirds, and is developed from, his earlier epistemological work. Again and again in his later writings Polanyi starts discussion of an issue from the generalisation of his analysis of a machine into two logical and ontological levels – showing how important he himself regarded this part of his work. God is to be seen as both occupying the level immediately above man's consciousness and will, and also as being present to all levels of our universe, holding them in being. It would be a great mistake to limit God to one transcendent level (which some of Polanyi's followers and commentators have shown a tendency to do), and even our language prevents us from doing so, for to speak of a 'transcendent' level is to modify and stretch our conception of a level in the hope that it can serve to enable us to say something about the mode of God's presence to his creation. God revealed in Jesus Christ is both the one in whom the whole universe 'lives and moves and has its being',[15] and the transcendent Creator with whom man alone within creation is capable of true inter-personal communion.

The most developed statement of Polanyi's articulation of God's interaction with the various levels of created reality is the important chapter in *Meaning* entitled *Order*. I would suggest that where in this chapter (and elsewhere in his writings) Polanyi refers to a field or gradient of potential meaning we should identify this with the living God, although we cannot reverse it and say that these fields *are* God, for God is far more than merely the fields of meaning present in and to creation. It is God who is at work evoking and sustaining the ever more meaningful organisations of matter which Polanyi describes.

Although this is the case, it is understandable that most of what occurs in the processes of life can be understood and classified by scientific investigation and explanation. God does not habitually play dice, to adapt Einstein's expression. It is worth noting here, as David Hume did long ago, a misunderstanding of the concept of natural law which is still widespread. Events in the world are not 'caused' by any law. The recognition of laws of created activity must always follow the existence of the events themselves. Michael Polanyi points this out even and especially in the case of such basic principles or laws as those of the equilibration of forces, which must be *assumed* before anything can be weighed.[16] Natural laws can only point us to God as the source of all law and order in the activity of creation. But they can in this way serve as genuine clues to God, as they evidently did for Polanyi himself. These clues do not constitute a second Bible. We can still only see the concealed divine government of the world by keeping tacitly in mind God's revealed activity in the history of Israel which was summed up in Jesus Christ. We must be content with this form of knowledge of God's action in the world.

Thus, if we cannot interpose an intermediary acting subject (a

Demiurge?) under the guise of 'law' or 'field' or 'reality' between God and individual events in the universe, we can only see every part of our life as lived directly before God. We have to do directly with God, and only indirectly with the laws of creation, so far as they are known to us. It is in God – and not merely somewhere near him – that we live and move and have our being.

Let us explore this a little further. How can we speak of the actions of two free subjects, God and man, being present in one action, an action of God's creation? How is it conceivable that the freedom of the one does not compromise the freedom of the other? The only way this is possible is if the two subjects operate on separate but co-ordinated levels, the one subject (man) with a necessary subordination, and the other subject (God) with a necessary superiority. Then the action of God and of man can be seen properly as one co-ordinated action. God's action does not lurk behind that of creation. It is God who speaks when the Old Testament Prophet speaks, and it is God who sends the sun and the rain on the just and the unjust. The finger of God is equally and generally omnipresent in sacred history and in the entire history of the world; the Bible makes no distinction here. The danger arises when a logical relation is posited between the activity of God and that of creation. This has the effect of destroying any recognition of the autonomy of the two levels. Rather curiously, this only arises when there is a need to bridge a previously posited dualistic gap between God and the world. Such a logical bridge soon becomes uncertain. For example, consider the effect of the Lisbon earthquake on the rationalistic belief in God expressed in the dualistic outlook of eighteenth-century Deism, or the attacks of Ockhamists and others on the Aristotelian logic used to connect God and the world in medieval Roman Catholic theology and cosmology. And where such a logical relation between God and creation is posited, man soon starts to see himself and even the inanimate creation around him as divine. We get an autonomous, secularised man believing and behaving as if he is God and therefore able to do just as he pleases.

We can avoid all these difficulties and consequences only if we ever keep in mind the fact that God is always the active but free Lord of creation. Thus the oneness of the action of God and man in creaturely activity can only be seen from the side of God – just as the oneness of the two natures of Jesus Christ can only be seen in the light of the divine nature and person of God.

This oneness of the action of God and man is difficult to grasp for us twentieth-century men. Creation is still contingent and free on this view. And if it is not fate or chance which determines what creation does, what is it? It must be God. Man will reap what he has sown, but the nature of that which he sows and reaps will be decided by God – for who else could decide? What greater honour could God give to his world than an appropriate place and share in his own activity, by making man's activity the means of his own activity? In this way creation will be seen to serve God compulsorily but not necessarily. All this may seem paradoxical – but I would suggest that we have here one of the paradoxes which Polanyi referred to as the happy dwelling places of the human mind.

If in created activity we have to do directly with God's sustaining power, we can immediately acknowledge that God can freely ignore the laws known to us. I refer of course to the possibility of miracles. Even then God does not act as a God of disorder, but as the God of his own inherent order, no matter how certain we may believe individual laws to be. We can recall in this connection Polanyi's lack of any sympathy for the view that our knowledge of the intelligibility and regularity of creation provided a shred of real evidence which could count against the existence of supernatural and miraculous activity by God in creation.[17] Naturally we constantly await the further refinement of our understanding of creaturely laws and norms; so we must hesitate before believing we have identified a particular example of this special activity of God. Yet it can be said to be hardly surprising, the more definitely the coming of Jesus Christ is announced in the Old Testament, and the more directly his revelation is attested in the New Testament, the more understandable it is to unprejudiced reason to believe that there were events in our world which occurred in violation of known laws of nature. The creation of heaven and earth at the beginning of time was an event of this character, and so will be the consummation of creation at the end of time as we know it. What is revealed in these events can hardly be described as miraculous exceptions but rather as the basic norm of divine activity, the law of God at which we are aiming with our concept of laws of nature and creation. Michael Polanyi has been of great help in enabling me to see how the inherently personal knowledge of natural science can complement but not rival the broader knowledge indicated by the Christian doctrine of providence.

I must stress that I have not 'answered' as such the old question of how God's free will and man's free will exist and combine. The mystery remains, as it is right that it should. My aim has rather been to show how we can dwell more deeply in this mystery and paradox.

As a former natural scientist myself, I find Michael Polanyi's thoughts on the need for a new theory of evolution exciting, especially because Darwin's theory has had and increasingly is having a profound influence in the modern world. The theory is atheistic.[18] In this context, however, I would only want to emphasise one interesting correlation. Polanyi points out[19] that the slow and long-range operations of evolution will not be noticed by the experimental geneticist or student of population genetics. Any indications of them are likely to be swamped by ephemeral genetic variations which are taking place, as it were, in the interstices of the dominant evolutionary trend. The same may be said of the comprehensive features of God's providence, of which the progress of evolution is an example. Often it will be only by looking back that we are able to see positive developments accruing from periods of history. There are numerous examples in the Bible of this retrospective recognition of God's action. For example, when the Old Testament asserts that 'God led Israel out of Egypt', or 'God spoke to Moses' we modern scientific men are apt to interpret such statements rather mechanically as if they are the observations of a modern journalist or historian. We are too ready to imagine in our minds a divine standard-bearer or a voice from the clouds! Rather they are to be seen as summary statements of a later age, referring to events which consisted of a whole series of individual events which at the time could have been interpreted in a number of ways.

Even the brief exposition of the Christian belief in divine providence attempted here could not be satisfactory unless we face another old question, that of the nature of the evil which seems to thwart God's good purposes. If God is so much in command of his world, then why is there so much evil and suffering and thus opposition to his good purposes? Although I cannot say much here on the subject, I must say something, for Michael Polanyi may have relevance here for Christian theology.

If we ask why creation or each of us has to be as it is, the only fundamentally correct answer is that if God is truly the Lord of creation it must be so by God's free will. If we ask the further question why creation has to be afflicted by sin, death and the devil, again we can only give the same answer that it is by the free will of God that evil is allowed its definite if peculiar place. And if we ask the further question why God chose to redeem his creation by incarnation and atonement, only the same answer can be given. Other ultimate questions could only receive similar answers. However, more can perhaps be said about the existence of evil – if with caution and reverence. We can, I think, say that God's supreme Good for creation comes properly to view not simply when the obedience and blessedness of the world are its self-evident nature and the simple fulfilment of its existence, but when they are salvation from the threatening presence of evil. In this way creation is constantly reminded that its goodness, meaning and intelligibility constantly depend on the God who gives all, to the point of the crucifixion, to maintain and preserve his world. If it is true that God is greater in the very fact that he is the God who opposes evil and sin and suffering, who forgives and saves from death, then can we complain about the strange existence in our midst of this evil? On this view evil only exists by virtue of God's disavowal and rejection of it. Precisely this rejection by God makes it utterly evil and demonic. Yet because it only exists in this way, evil too is under God's control and government. There is no sphere of being or non-being which is not in its own way subject to the will of God – for such a sphere would inevitably be that of another God.

We are faced here with the mystery of the Cross, for it is only in the light of God wrestling with evil to the point of the crucifixion of God incarnate who was the one perfectly obedient and therefore sinless man, that we see the abysmal reality of evil. And it is only in the resurrection that we see the triumph of God over that which he detests and rejects. I do not want to suggest that evil disappears in some compensating harmony, yet against that view I cannot but see evil as stripped of its *ultimate* power by the action of God in Jesus Christ.

Can we relate this to Michael Polanyi's understanding of the presence of failure at all levels, mechanical, biological and moral, in the universe? Characteristically Polanyi starts here by analysing the relationship between the two levels of reality present in a machine, and concludes: 'The operational principles of machines are rules of rightness, which account only for the successful working of machines but leave their failures entirely unexplained. When a boiler bursts, a crankshaft snaps, or a train is derailed, these things behave against the rules laid down for them within the conception of a machine'.[20] Accordingly, as Polanyi points out, there are in a strict sense no *reasons* for the failure of a machine, but only *causes* due to the physical components of the machine not possessing the appropriate physical or chemical characteristics to satisfy the boundary conditions defined for the successful operation of the machine. Conversely, there are *reasons* but not *causes* for the successful operation of a machine. 'If a stratagem succeeds, it does so in accordance with its own premeditated internal reasons; if it fails, this is due to unforeseen external causes'.[21] This analysis of Polanyi's applies to genuine machines. A badly designed machine fails because a consequence or aspect of its poor design is the lack of availability of materials of the correct physical and chemical properties for it to succeed. A perpetual motion machine fails because the materials of nature are never frictionless. And although a person's bodily functions may be restored to health by a change of climate, the change of climate only alters the conditions on which the body itself relies for its healthy operation. A good climate, or nourishing food, cannot of itself explain good health.

Extending and generalising his analysis of a machine, Michael Polanyi describes the hierarchy of levels present in living beings: 'The lowest functions of life are those called vegetative; these vegetative functions, sustaining life at its lowest level, leave open – in both plants and animals – the higher functions of growth, and leave open in animals also the operations of muscular action; next in turn, the principles governing muscular action in animals leave open the integration of such action to innate patterns of behaviour; and again such patterns are open in their turn to be shaped by intelligence; while the workings of intelligence itself can be made to serve in man the still higher principles of responsible choice'.[22] At each level there exist higher powers for attaining deeper meaning, yet at the same time there are new possibilities of corruption. Plants are subject to malformation and disease, animals to illusion and error, and finally in man, in addition to all these liabilities, an ingrained propensity to commit moral evil. 'Such is the necessary condition of a morally responsible being, grafted on a bestiality through which alone it can exercise its own powers.'[23]

Polanyi equates this with 'The inescapable predicament of man which theology has called his fallen nature'.[24] Here he seems to be saying in an illuminating way the same thing I have suggested that theology does on its own ground. The failures of creation at its various levels (from earthquakes to sin) are an indirect result of the presence of meaningful operational principles or rules of rightness. As a form or effect of evil, failure does not exist *per se*. But just as there are no rational reasons but only lower-level causes for failure, so God should not be seen as the active author of evil. Moreover, the good that we as human beings do must be ascribed to the level above us, the transcendent 'level' discussed earlier, which is God. As the New Testament puts it, even when we do all that we can, we must regard ourselves as unprofitable servants.[25] We must, however, guard ourselves on the opposite side as well. Just as we do not see God as the author of evil, neither must we regard God's creation as evil in itself. If this were the case then our vision of redemption would be a bodiless, spiritual hereafter quite unconnected to our present world. This means, then, that we are not to think of our multi-levelled existence as inherently evil, but rather as inescapably *prone* to evil in its present state of expectation. I am sure that Michael Polanyi would recognise the importance of this distinction, although on occasions he could speak rather ambiguously of the ultimate and eternal future for creation and the human race in particular. His most direct statements come (to the best of my knowledge) in his essay *Faith and Reason*. Here he faces the question of the relation between a person and his body, and categorically rejects the idea that a person can exist outside his body. At this point he explicitly recognises his startling proximity to the Christian doctrines of incarnation and atonement achieved in and by Jesus Christ and declared in his bodily resurrection from the dead as the pledge of our future resurrection. Polanyi's vision is thus of the redemption of this world and these bodies of ours. The risen Jesus still bears the marks of the Cross, as the New Testament makes clear.

It must be emphasised that I do not want to dissolve or resolve either the mystery of evil or the corresponding mystery of redemption by incarnation and atonement. All I suggest is that in Polanyi's analysis of the asymmetry of success and failure in levels above the lowest, that occupied by physics and chemistry, we see a possible analogy to the status of evil in relation to God. Associated with this we can perhaps see a clue to the inherent logic of the incarnation and atonement of Jesus Christ.

Prayer

What relevance does this understanding of providence have for the active Christian life? It certainly must be said that the Christian believer is still a creature, and that in solidarity with all other men and creatures he stands wholly under the lordship of God. This carries with it the same disadvantage for every man or every insect, that he cannot be his own Lord and must therefore always be subject to risk and doubt in all he does. But it also carries with it the same advantage, that he need not ultimately worry that all is absurd or meaningless and thus destined for extinction. Yet in distinction from all other creatures, man is asked as a potentially and therefore actually responsible subject to say yes or no to being a creature under the sole and universal lordship of God. The Christian explicitly says yes, lays aside any claims to self-glory and allows himself to be moulded by the glorious grace of his active Lord. Whereas other men may see little or no, or rather an ambiguous and uncertain, purpose operating in the history of the universe, the Christian sees in it the omnipotent lordship of the Creator and Redeemer. This in turn means that the Christian is able to participate outwardly and actively and to some extent inwardly in the providential Lordship of God. The Christian is the true creature, just as Jesus Christ was the revelation of true humanity. We can express this in various ways, each having its validity and its dangers. We may say that the Christian co-operates on his own level and in his own place with God. We may follow the New Testament and refer to Christians as friends and co-workers with God. Whatever terminology we favour, the essential point is to compromise neither the intimate and inner nature of God's presence in us, e.g. 'It is no longer I who live, but Christ who lives in me',[26] nor the direct address of God to the responsible man, e.g. 'Be reconciled to God'[27]. The truth lies with integrating intuitively into a joint meaning these seemingly incompatible elements in the paradox of Christian existence.

What can this mean concretely for the Christian? In the broadest terms, we can take up St. Paul's claim that the three basic attitudes or attributes of a true man are faith, love and hope. Faith has here a certain primacy, not in importance or in time, but as describing the basic Christian attitude of acknowledging the truth involved in being human. It is the confidence with which the Christian trusts his Creator and Lord. As such it embraces the whole man, and is altogether the work of man, but is awakened, evoked or prompted by the living God whose work on the higher level it also is. Faith both totally enslaves and totally liberates the true man. In this the Christian feels one with Jesus Christ who in his very being is true God and true man. The Christian dwells in his Lord, which expression again brings the thought of Polanyi and St. Paul and the Gospel of John into a close relationship. If the Christian dwells in his Lord in this way, he must spontaneously and naturally imitate his Lord's life of obedience and love. The real vision of God which faith is involves the necessary corresponding action.

There is an immediate analogy here with Michael Polanyi's description of scientific discovery. Belief in the truth, or rather in the intimation of truth, in a particular scientific theory is not the product of a deliberate act of the will, but of the scientist waking up to an insight. 'No labour can make a discovery, but no discovery can be made without intense, absorbing, devoted labour.'[28] Similarly the faith of a Christian is not a product of his love and obedience, but is impossible without the costly and self-sacrificing cultivation and practise of his love and obedience. This to some extent is the resolution of the long controversy over the relation between faith and works.

How is the hope of the Christian expressed? It is certainly no afterthought to faith and love, but just as God is three in one and one in three, so are faith, love and hope distinguished and related. Hence, just as in our faith and love we dwell in our Lord, so also in our hope we dwell in the God revealed in Jesus Christ. God is the hope of man. He revealed himself as such by dying with us and for us. For this reason faith, love and hope can only issue in prayer as the concrete action demanded of man by God at this point. In prayer a man lays aside his relationships within the world and looks only to God. In faith, love and hope a man is also directly before God. But the Christian can never simply assume that he has the insight and power for genuine hope, love and obedience. And the faith in which alone he can be obedient in love and hope is not so readily available that he has only to remind himself and he will believe afresh. In prayer man presents himself to God, the God whom he can always think he is avoiding in the worldly activities of life, but is unable to avoid in any part of his life, and asks that he may be given the faith and love and hope which he needs. Man prays that his whole life may yet again be renewed in spite of all his past failings. The confession of these failings and thanksgiving for their forgiveness will obviously be elements in Christian prayer. In the form of a direct approach to God, prayer will be the action of faith, love and hope *par excellence*, the action from which all the other actions of the Christian must spring. The source of the Christian's strength can only be God.

If we were to leave the description and analysis of prayer at this point, however, we would be in danger of not seeing it as an activity with its own reality. It might simply merge into faith and love and hope, or into an act of worship. It is all these but more. In the New Testament the decisive element in prayer is asking, petition. The Lord's prayer materially consists of six petitions. This is what distinguishes the worship and prayer of the Christian from a mere glancing upwards in reverence before the numinous. 'Ask and you will receive', as the New Testament bluntly puts it, for in prayer a Christian does not ask vacantly, expecting an answer only on rare occasions. I shall return to the obvious question concerning the answering of prayer which arises here. But first let us ask what is the inner reason for the centrality of asking in Christian prayer.

It is not simply that God is so rich and powerful and we are so poor and powerless, true though this is. For that is only relevant in the light of the more basic factor revealed in the New Testament, namely that God has drawn so near to us that we can only see our situation as that of children before their Father. It is this nearness of the Creator and Redeemer that is specifically and distinctively Christian. This is the content of the revelation of God in Jesus Christ. It is on this basis that we can put behind and away from us any fear on our part in coming before God. The richness and power of God are not against us but with us. The Christian is able to ask and receive precisely because God gives himself and all that he possesses. St. Paul puts this succinctly: 'He who did not spare his own Son but gave him up for us all, will he not also give us all things with him'?[29]

To understand what is involved it is necessary to emphasise the order in which St. Paul puts this. However strange it may initially sound, God really hears and answers our prayers in Jesus Christ. St. Paul is unequivocal about this. Out of the fullness of this basic answer we find our own prayers answered. It is his light which falls on every man and all creation.[30] The Christian dwells in this divine answer to all prayer. The Christian as a member of the body of Christ here on earth does not pray alone; Christ prays with him, even as he first prayed his own Lord's prayer with his disciples. In putting complete trust in Jesus Christ, the Christian loses his life only to find it again. This is very much how Michael Polanyi expressed the action of the dedicated human being in search of truth, especially once he has intimations that he is on the right track. The scientist assumes that creation is intelligible before he puts questions (in the form of experiments) to it. Similarly, the Christian can only assume that God answers prayer before he prays. The Christian is able to lose himself in Jesus Christ only to find himself again because God's purpose in creating the universe was his Son's becoming man for its salvation. The Christian praying in the world is face to face with its inner mystery. Furthermore, just as Jesus Christ does not exist as man simply for himself but for the world, so the Christian is not called simply for his own sake but for the sake of the world. Christians are the salt of the earth. For this reason, at bottom the asking of Christian prayer is asking for the world which does not itself pray. The Christian exists, with his Lord but under him, to witness to the world and to intercede for it in order to share the witness and intercession of Christ. This asking of the Church gives expression to the inarticulate groaning of creation.[31] The order of the requests in the Lord's prayer is important here. The Christian first asks that God's will be done on earth, and thus that his kingdom should come, before he asks for the food and forgiveness which will enable him to participate in the work of God.

Participation in the work of God is the heart of the matter, and the key to our understanding the 'difficulties' so often referred to in books on prayer. The basic difficulty we all have with prayer is that of all human activities it is the one where we are called upon most to set aside our lower selfish nature. Naturally we all find this difficult! We are only human! For the same reason we have difficulty in loving truly, that is, truly selflessly. Only when actively we lose ourselves in imitating and participating in the prayer life of the one truly faithful and loving human who was also God can we really pray. As in the more general case of the providential activity of God, here too we have to see in prayer the action of God and man occurring in a co-ordinated if differentiated unity. The New Testament can speak of the Holy Spirit being sent into our hearts to enable us to pray.[32] Left to ourselves our prayer is weak and impotent, and hence God mercifully comes to the aid of our prayer. In prayer it is a question of two basic levels, our inadequate and subordinate level, and God's omniscient and omnipotent love. This dual nature in the Christian understanding of prayer is finely expressed by St. Paul: 'I will pray with the Spirit, and I will pray with the mind also'.[33]

To face the chief intellectual difficulty: how can it be that the individual prayers of believers are heard and answered? Does this not imply that God is conditioned by our prayers? Yes! The Bible is quite unambiguous about this. Prayer is always answered. The living God is not an irresistible fate before which man can only keep silent and passive. Christian resignation, as opposed to true Christian patience and waiting, is based on unbelief concerning this living God. The profundity of God's lordship is such that he allows us a place in his government of the world. Here below, on our level, we co-operate with God as his friend and co-worker. This, I take it, is at least part of the meaning of the passage: 'I shall give you the keys of the kingdom of heaven, and whatever you bind on earth shall be bound in heaven, and whatever you shall loose on earth shall be loosed in heaven'.[34] This points to the seriousness of our actions as Christians. It does not mean that we hold the reins of world government. They are in the hands of God. But we have our place in their exercise. In his supreme omnipotence and omniscience God wills to share his life with us. This means that true Christian prayer cannot imply any tyranny, divine or human. It is only the prayer which shares the characteristic of that in Gethsemane: 'Not my will, but thy will be done', which will be answered in the manner anticipated by the one who prays. Thus it need hardly be said that God will rectify and amend our prayer in his answering of it. It is not as if our prayer is the certain and secure thing, and God's answer unsure and uncertain. It is the opposite. It is we who are challenged in prayer, not God. The trouble is that we are so used to thinking in terms of what seems tangible to us that when we think of prayer we all too easily start by thinking of the particular words we speak or think. This is a reductionist approach. In prayer we look beyond the level of our words to their truth which can only come from God.

This situation can be illustrated by a further consideration of the nature of the power given to the Church to forgive sins. According to St. Matthew the saying about the keys of the kingdom is specifically directed to Peter in one passage[35], but to all the disciples in another.[36] According to St. John, who reports it as directed to all the disciples, the saying is adapted to refer explicitly to the forgiving of sins: 'If you forgive the sins of any, they are forgiven; if you retain the sins of any, they are retained'.[37] The contexts of all three verses refer to the nature of the mission of the Church. We can immediately reject the perverse interpretation given to these verses by some past and present church-men wherein it is thought that the Church has the option of choosing the negative alternative. Jesus was not commanding his disciples to imitate the action of the scribes, Pharisees and lawyers who prevented men from entering the Kingdom of Heaven.[38] Am I correct, however, to suggest that the power to forgive or, if the Church fails in its mission, not to forgive sins is none other than the power of prayer? Is there not the possibility of another more direct power given to the Church and its representatives in their power to forgive sins? If the Church is not infallible, then it is reasonable to reject such a possibility. The power of the Church is the power of prayer – a power which is endowed with the certainty of God's answer. These verses indicate, therefore, that in the manifold activity of the Church, all of which bears the character of prayer, the invasion of earth by the Kingdom of Heaven is either advanced or hindered. God is either glorified or shamed by the work of the Church, by its lawful releasing of sins or its unlawful binding of sins. This is true because God has genuinely made his cause that of his Church also. If God is not bound to what the Church on earth does or does not do, he certainly participates most intimately in it. The participation by God in the affairs of the Church puts a direct challenge to the Church: is it facilitating the forgiveness of sins and the establishment on earth of the Kingdom of Heaven? This challenge is analogous to that posed by God to the prayers of the individual believer.

I have said that God is conditioned by our prayer. To say this is of course to stretch the meaning of our language. If indeed God is conditioned by our prayer he is not basically altered by it. What else is revealed when God hears and answers prayer but that he is the Creator and Lord of all things? And how can his lordship over man, his free creature, be more gloriously revealed than by his taking seriously man's requests? This may seem inconceivable, but what is truly inconceivable is the incarnation of God in Jesus Christ as the fundamental declaration of the extent to which God takes man and human activity seriously. We cannot prove by recourse to experiment or theoretical deduction that God answers prayer any more than we can prove the existence of God by such means. Jesus never argued for the validity of prayer any more than he argued for the existence of God. To have done so would have appeared presumptuous and blasphemous. God, and prayer to God, were for Jesus the beginning and end of experience. Because Jesus was himself God we can immediately see that prayer is part of the very life of the triune God. It might seem incompatible that God should pray to God, but if we start to think this we should ask ourselves whether we are not making the error of defining God in terms of a natural or anthropomorphic conception of prayer. Rather we should take such apparent incompatibles as clues to help us apprehend something of the inner richness of the being and life of God. The validity of prayer can only rest on the infinite love of God which allows the existence of parallel seemingly incompatible features of creation in the prayers of Christians. That God is affected by our prayers does not emphasise the finitude or anthropomorphic nature of his love, but rather his selfless infinity. The rough features of prayer illustrate apparent incompatibles. In praying we find both confrontation by God and co-operation with him. On the one hand, we are confronted by God and moved to praise, thanksgiving and penitence. On the other hand, we are moved to co-operate with God in petition and intercession.

In attempting to understand and accept that God does indeed answer prayer it helps to recognise that there can be no ulterior motives for prayer. We should not pray simply because we want to relieve anxiety. Prayer is not begging in the hope of unexpected and intermittent rewards. If the question 'What is the use of prayer?' means only 'Does it produce the goods requested according to human judgment?' we have abandoned God for the theology of the market-place.[39] Sadly, this is an all too common view of prayer. We pray because this is the action demanded of us by God if we are to fulfil our dependence upon and inter-relation with him. Michael Polanyi expressed the same view in regard to belief in God: 'Suppose it were decided by psychiatrists that a general increase in psychoneurotic ailments could only be checked by a restoration of religious faith; this would not make us all believe in God. In fact no ulterior advantage can make us believe in God, while if we do believe in God no consequent disadvantage can make us lose our faith. Ulterior motives will never produce genuine belief'.[40]

This can be expressed in another way. In prayer we cannot bypass the crucifixion. In looking to the Cross in our prayerful search for God and response to him, we are simultaneously questioned and comforted. In the Cross we see dramatically declared the fact that our only hope lies in God and therefore not as such in our decision to pray or in the content of our prayers. At the same time we are also comforted, for if God has endured the Cross for us, what need we fear? This I take it is Polanyi's meaning in that haunting passage from *Personal Knowledge*: 'Christian worship sustains, as it were, an eternal, never to be consummated hunch: a heuristic vision which is accepted for the sake of its unresolvable tension. It is like an obsession with a problem known to be insoluble, which yet follows, against reason, unswervingly, the heuristic command: 'Look at the unknown!' Christianity sedulously fosters, and in a sense permanently satisfies, man's craving for mental dissatisfaction by offering him the comfort of a crucified God'.[41]

The key to our understanding of the docrines of providence and prayer lies in our doctrine of God. Far too often in our Western

129

tradition we have been content with a view of God which imprisoned him in his own simplicity and self-determination. Down at the roots of our thinking – roots of which we are often unaware, but which are all the more influential for that – there lurks the thought that God is in some sense bound to his lonely eternity. Strictly speaking, this view of God is anthropomorphic, in the bad sense of that word. It is arrived at by critical reflection on what creation is not. It identifies God with a simple, unmoved philosophical Absolute whose omnipotence is naked power and whose onmiscience is fatalism. This view can often approximate to the equation of God with death. This view to a large extent underlay the 'God of the gaps' and 'God is dead' controversies. We can often forget that it was in the name of such a monotheism that Jesus Christ was rejected and crucified. We must take God as the source and standard of all that is real, and reject the opposite and anthropomorphic procedure which defines God in terms of what we observe and feel to be real in our experience. God is richer and more personal than we are in his life as Father, Son and Holy Spirit.

Michael Polanyi said comparatively little about prayer and our concept of God. He spoke of prayer as a supreme act of trust that what may not appear to be happening in the world, God's government of it, is actually taking place. He spoke of God as 'The focal point that fuses into meaning all the incompatibles involved in the practice of religion . . . and in this way God also becomes the integration of all the incompatibles in our own lives'.[42] These brief and ambiguous statements of his could be seen as expanded and given more contour in the traditional formulations as I have outlined them. Polanyi's God was certainly intimately involved in all that occurs in the world, without thereby being resolved into the activity of the world as the modern process theologians would seem to advocate. My attempt has been to render plausible an integration of the type Polanyi suggests is necessary, with particular reference to the Christian doctrines of providence and prayer.

NOTES TO CHAPTER 6

1. Michael Polanyi and Harry Prosch, *Meaning*, p. 180.
2. Michael Polanyi, *Personal Knowledge*, p. 381.
3. *Personal Knowledge*, p. 381.
4. *Science, Faith and Society*, p. 84.
5. *The Tacit Dimension*, p. 92.

6. J. H. Newman, *The Grammar of Assent*, 2nd Edit., p. 55.

7. See, for example, ch. 7 of *Personal Knowledge*, pp. 203ff; Part one of *Knowing and Being*, pp. 3ff.; and ch. 1 of *Meaning*, pp. 3ff.

8. I am here adapting an important element of Polanyi's thought. For the distinction between *focal* and *subsidiary* awareness see p. 137.

9. This expression of Polanyi's is taken from the final two sentences of *Personal Knowledge*, p. 405: 'We may envisage then a cosmic field which called forth all these centres of thought – i.e. by human beings by offering them a short-lived, limited, hazardous opportunity for making some progress of their own towards an unthinkable consummation. And that is also, I believe, how a Christian is placed when worshipping God'.

10. In modern usage, the concept 'lord' can be taken in a variety of quite different senses. Here I am referring to the Biblical notion of an active Creator and Redeemer who is both loving and righteous. This is the active Lord who will intervene on behalf of mankind to the point of laying down his incarnate life for his beloved creation.

11. For a full explanation of Polanyi's use of this expression, see, for example, ch. 2 of *The Tacit Dimension*.

12. It is significant that the New Testament 'reality' and 'truth' are merged in one word, *aletheia*, which has a living and self-disclosing aspect. Hence the centrality of the claim of Jesus: 'I am the truth' (St. John 14.6). It is such an active, self-revealing concept of 'reality' which Polanyi developed.

13. *Personal Knowledge*, p. 324.

14. This is a crucial concept in Polanyi's thought. It is given an early presentation in ch. 11 of *Personal Knowledge*, and Polanyi expands it at many points in his later writings – for example, see ch. 2 of *The Tacit Dimension*, or ch. 13 of *Knowing and Being*. It does *not* imply a hierarchy of Being in a Neoplatonic or pantheistic sense. It refers to an ontology of created being, not of the Being of God.

15. The Acts of the Apostles, 17.28.

16. Michael Polanyi and Harry Prosch, *Meaning*, p. 174f.

17. *Personal Knowledge*, p. 284.

18. It may be argued that no scientific theory can be either theistic or atheistic, but I would dissent from such a view. It is the presupposition that the only forces at work in evolution are random mutation and natural selection that makes the theory reductionist and therefore atheistic. Polanyi knew this. He remarks (*Personal Knowledge*, p. 383) concerning the neo-Darwinian theory of evolution: 'There is some fundamental principle missing'. In ch. 11 of *Meaning* he enlarges and develops his important arguments for the inadequacy of the neo-Darwinian theory of evolution and its accompanying assumption that life can be explained wholly in terms of physics and chemistry.

19. *Personal Knowledge*, p. 385.

20. *Personal Knowledge*, p. 329.

21. *Personal Knowledge*, p. 332.

22. *Personal Knowledge*, p. 358.

23. 'Faith and Reason', in *Scientific Thought and Social Reality*, p. 129. Cf. *Personal Knowledge*, p. 334.

24. *Ibid.*

131

25. St. Luke 17.10.
26. Galatians 2.20.
27. 2 Corinthians 5.20
28. Michael Polanyi, *Scientific Thought and Social Reality*, p. 129.
29. Romans 8.32.
30. St. John 1.9.
31. Romans 8.22.
32. Romans 8.15f, 26; Galatians 4.6.
33. 1 Corinthians 14.15.
34. St. Matthew 16.19.
35. St. Matthew 16.19.
36. St. Matthew 18.18.
37. St. John 20.23.
38. St. Matthew 23.13; St. Luke 11.52.
39. I have adapted the illustration from P. R. Baelz, *Prayer and Providence*, p. 30.
40. Michael Polanyi, *Personal Knowledge*, p. 183.
41. *Personal Knowledge*. p. 199.
42. *Meaning*, p. 156.

NOTES ON TERMS
AND CONCEPTS

THOMAS F. TORRANCE

abstraction – a mode of thought in which the observable surface of
something is considered apart from the concrete base in reality to
which it is naturally joined, or in which certain aspects of reality
are subjected to attention to the neglect of all others. Traditionally the purpose of abstraction is to separate the essential features
exhibited by a set of particular things in order to reach a general
conception of them as a class, or to detach the formal aspects of
things from their material embodiment so that they can be more
easily and consistently connected together in a formal system.
Abstraction thus imposes on thought a dualism between form
and matter or structure and being which gives rise to a formalistic and artificial picture of things. The highly formalised and
mechanised conception of the world deriving from classical
(Newtonian) physics suffers from extensive abstraction of this
kind.

abstractive knowledge – the knowledge by which something is apprehended not as it is in itself but only through the forms in which it
appears to us.

accrediting – to acknowledge the valid claims of something to have
meaning or value, in such a way as to entrust ourselves to its
acceptance. Accrediting is a form of appraisal with commitment.

articulate/inarticulate – beyond common linguistic usage, this pair
of terms is used by Polanyi to refer to expressible and in-
expressible acts of intelligence which are deeply interconnected.
All acts of thinking or knowing are rooted in and rely on in-
expressible or inarticulate operations of the mind and can never
supersede them.

axioms – the ultimate suppositions on which scientific knowledge
rests, for which no proof can be offered other than their self-
evidence. Axioms like definitions cannot be completely formulated, for any formulation or definition must refer to other

axioms or terms. In addition to basic axioms there are also operative axioms, the working premises of a science which are founded on basic axioms. This distinction corresponds to that between ultimate and working beliefs.

boundary conditions – (an expression borrowed from physics) the set of requirements imposed on one level of reality where it borders on another. It is through boundary conditions that the organisational principles at one level are left open to control (at least in part) by the operational principles of a higher level, but the latter cannot be accounted for by the principles governing the particulars which constitute the next-lower level. Thus the mind relies for its working on the continued operation of physiological principles, but it controls the boundary conditions left undetermined by physiology. A boundary condition is always extraneous to the process which it delimits.

commitment – the personal and responsible submission of the mind to the requirements of a reality independent of it. Commitment expresses a belief on the strength of which a person is prepared to entrust himself to the claims of reality upon him. Unlike its popular use, commitment, in Polanyi's thought, is not a subjective state, for it 'purposely' refers the self away to what is independent of it. Commitment is objectively, not subjectively, oriented.

comprehension – in Polanyi's particular use, the act of understanding whereby disjoined particulars are grasped in a comprehensive whole. Comprehension is an integrative, not an analytical, act of knowledge, but it can never be wholly explicit and therefore remains necessarily incomplete. In traditional theology, comprehension is often distinguished from apprehension. To comprehend something is to grasp it in its totality, to contain the whole of it in thought; to apprehend something is to grasp it only in part, i.e. to grasp something that exceeds the power of the mind to contain it within the bounds of its thought. God may be apprehended but not comprehended. We may grasp him only with open concepts for all our concepts of him are inadequate and fall short of his full reality.

conviviality – the interpersonal relations of a community in tacit sharing of basic convictions which underly all articulate consensus and communication; the conjoint knowing of living beings which undergirds a common frame of mind in experience and knowing. It is through the process of convivial knowing (akin to empathy) that there is a continuous transition from the natural sciences to the humanities and from both to the knowledge of the Person of God. The counterpart to conviviality in Christian experience is Eucharistic Fellowship, or, more generally, communion (*koinonia*).

cosmology – the meaning of the universe as a whole, or theory of the universe of space and time as an ordered totality and understood in terms of its immanent laws. This may take the form of a general (philosophical or religious) outlook, or the form of a scientific account of the origin and structure of the universe.

definition – a precise statement determining the exact nature or meaning of something. Every definition of one set of terms relies on other undefined terms to explain them. Expressed the other way round, a definition is the tacit reliance on one set of terms to make precise the meaning of another set of terms. Hence any interpretation of a definition must rely on its undefined understanding by the person making it.

detachment – a dispassionate mode of thought unaffected by prior beliefs or subjective prejudices. Complete detachment, according to Polanyi, is a false ideal, for it is only attachment to the nature of what we seek to know that detaches us from false assumptions. Properly, detachment means commitment to a particular approach deemed to be appropriate to the occasion and disengagement from other points of view which for the time being are inadmissible.

discovery – the acquisition of new knowledge which could not be inferred from what we already know. Scientific discovery is an inexact operation, for it is more a skill and an art relying on unspecifiable clues and personal judgment, than a routine mode of learning. Discovery is made through active inquiry, following up an anticipatory recognition of a real coherence in nature, in which we seek to let the reality concerned disclose itself to us in its own intrinsic intelligibility.

dual control – any complex system is subject to control on two levels. While the lower level is controlled by the laws governing its constituent elements, it is also controlled by being subject through its boundary conditions to determination by the laws governing the higher level. Thus both machines and living organisms are subject to dual control by the laws of physics and chemistry at one level, and by engineering principles or biological operations at another level. Moreover, each level is said to be subject to dual control by the laws applying to its component particulars in themselves and by the laws that control the comprehensive entity formed by them. Polanyi also speaks of this as the principle of marginal or boundary control.

dualism – the division of reality into two incompatible spheres of being. This may be cosmological, in the dualism between a sensible and an intelligible realm, neither of which can be reduced to the other. It may also be epistemological, in which the empirical and theoretical aspects of reality are separated from one another, thereby giving rise to the extremes of empiricism and rationalism. It may also be anthropological, in a dualism between the mind and the body, in which a physical and a mental substance are conceived as either interacting with one another or as running a parallel course without affecting one another. In the Judaeo-Christian tradition man is regarded as an integrated whole, who is soul of his body and body of his soul. See *mind/ body 'dualism'*.

empiricism – an exclusively empirical approach to knowledge which rejects any form of intuitive apprehension of reality beyond the range of the senses or what can be deduced from the immediate data of sense experience. 'Linguistic' empiricism holds that all statements depend for their meaning on sense experience alone. 'Scientific' empiricism limits knowledge to explicit, empirically verifiable, concepts and statements; it rejects all unprovable ideas or beliefs that transcend observable, tangible facts and thus rejects all knowledge of the higher intangible, invisible levels of existence.

epistemology – theory of knowledge concerned with the nature, source, range and validity of knowledge. Basic to Polanyi's epistemology is the bearing of knowing upon being, and its personal character, i.e. the role of the person as a rational centre in distinguishing what he knows from his knowing of it, and in the appraisal of order in reality and of the unspecifiable acts of recognition and discovery. See *personal knowledge*.

fiduciary act – act of faith or personal commitment such as pertains to scientific inquiry in the reliance upon coherence and meaning in that which we believe to exist. Far from implying any scepticism, scientific inquiry depends upon firm beliefs grounded in reality, and implies involvement rather than detachment.

focal/subsidiary – two kinds of awareness, focal by 'attending to' and subsidiary by 'relying on'. Focal awareness is of an object as an integrated whole, in reliance upon subsidiary awareness of its separated parts. There can be focal and subsidiary awareness of the same items but no awareness can be completely focal. To be aware of something subsidiarily is not to be aware of it in itself but only as a clue or an instrument pointing beyond itself. Subsidiaries function by being integrated to a focus on which they bear. For example, the words of a sentence refer thought to something independent of them; the use of a pair of stereo pictures focusses attention on their joint image. The same applies to tools, machines, etc. We are subsidiarily aware of a hammer in our hand when driving in a nail, or of a stick in probing the interior of a hidden cavity.

formal/informal – formal and informal elements are required for all rational speech and thought. While formal instruments of knowledge (grammar, logic, mathematics) greatly increase the range of our mental powers, formalisation necessarily remains incomplete, for it can never supersede but must continue to rely on informal acts of intelligence. It is the informal element which enables a formal system to be used meaningfully. It is impossible to reduce to formalism the bearing of forms of thought on being, or to incorporate into a formalisation rules for its interpretation and application. No system of rules, grammatical, logical or mathematical, can prescribe the procedure by which the rules themselves are to be understood and used. Words and concepts through long usage have a depth and a significance that can never be made wholly explicit. We always know more than we can tell, and our true statements (those bearing on reality) indicate more than they can express.

Gestalt – a German term for an automatically perceived pattern or configuration whose component parts are spontaneously organised into a coherent whole, e.g. in hearing a tune or recognising a face. In its origin Gestalt is a psychological percept, that which appears to the perceiver rather than something having independent reality in itself. Polanyi takes his cue from Gestalt psychology in developing his concept of comprehension of a coherent entity in which we are subsidiarily aware of particulars within our focal awareness of the entity as a whole. He differs from Gestalt psychology in that it fails to reckon with the intentional effort in perceiving, which is open to training (e.g. with respect to appraisal and judgment), and fails to reckon with the external manifestation of Gestalt which has an 'ontological' structure which can be 'logically' analysed and tested. Thus Polanyi rejects the phenomenalist assumptions behind the psychological analysis. His own concern with the ontological structure of perception is its affinity with the structure of scientific discovery, for which he offers neither a logical nor a psychological but an epistemic account. Discovery is a highly skilled activity dependent on personal powers of thought, both in the scientist's intuitive apprehension of a coherent outline or pattern in nature, and in his use of it as a clue in subsequent inquiry into the hitherto unknown reality which has given him that anticipatory intimation of its presence. Scientific knowledge advances through the discerning and exploring of Gestalten that are aspects of reality.

hermeneutics (from the Greek *hermeneus*, interpreter) – the activity of understanding and interpreting some subject-matter which is laden with meaning or information – of special importance in human and theological sciences. Hermeneutics is concerned with the elucidation, not so much of syntactical or logical relations, as of semantic relations, that is, with the bearing of forms of speech and thought upon the realities they indicate. In Polanyi's thought interpretation seeks to penetrate into the organic substructure of knowledge upon which explicit forms of thought and speech rely for their meaningful integration, and is specifically related to the transition from inarticulate learning to its articulate counterpart.

heuristics (from the Greek *heuriskein*, to find out, discover or invent) – a heuristic act is a fresh movement of thought serving the art of discovery or the solution of a problem; heuristic power is the capacity of some form or instrument of thought to give rise to additional knowledge. In heuristic activity the mind through an intuitive leap of insight and imagination crosses a 'logical gap' separating it from a hidden reality. This is an unaccountable act but it is not a blind leap, for it takes its rise from an element of foreknowledge which guides it. While heuristic activity operates from an anticipatory frame of thought it is an act of discovery breaking out of it which involves an irreversible modification of prior knowledge.

138

indwelling – more than the phenomenologists' notion of empathy, for it is the act of knowing in which we gain new meaning in the natural as well as the human sciences. It is the activity of knowing whereby the mind dwells in a coherence or integration latent in some object (or teaching or person) in order to interiorise it until there is a structural kinship between the knowing subject and the object known. In this way the natural integration in the object known is so assimilated into the knower that it functions as the subsidiary term in his focal understanding of it. Theologically regarded, indwelling is an act meditation and worship in and through which we are given access to God in his own inner communion.

integration – the natural unification of the constituent parts of a complex entity into a comprehensive whole, which is not replaced by an explicit integration or logical ordering of its analytically dismembered parts. Integration has to do with the spontaneous organisation of natural coherences embedded in nature, which we grasp or understand only through non-analytical acts of knowledge such as indwelling. In this way we accomplish mentally, in bringing subsidiaries to bear upon a focus, what living beings do physically. Integrative knowing is a unifying mode of thought in which we seek to grasp something by penetrating into its inner intelligible relations and wholeness without distorting fragmentation of it.

intuition – not the supreme immediate knowledge called 'intuition' by Leibniz or Spinoza or Husserl, but the inexplicable apprehension or insight into hidden coherences or intelligible order, which is indispensable at all stages of establishing knowledge, in discovery and in verification. According to Polanyi, the structure of scientific intuition is the same as that of perception, for it involves the same spontaneous process of sensing and integrating clues in response to some aspect of reality seeking realisation in our minds. This intuition of the relation between observation and reality is a faculty that can range over all grades of sagacity, from the highest level in the inspired guesses of scientific genius down to the minimum required for ordinary perception.

mechanistic world view – a conception of the universe in which all phenomena are explained exclusively in terms of their quantifiable properties and are mathematically systematised in accordanced with Newton's laws of motion. This is based on the conviction that in the last analysis nature consists of tiny entities which are externally connected to one another through strictly causal relations into a closed mechanical system. Polanyi objects to this mechanistic or deterministic view of the universe on the ground that by separating mathematics from natural processes it imposes a rigid artificial framework on everything which makes nonsense of our most vital experiences, for it constructs a view of the world, and develops a notion of science itself, in which mind is missing, purpose is excluded and meaning is denied.

mind/body 'dualism' – mind and body are related in such a way that the mind relies for its workings on the continued operations of physiological principles, but it controls the boundary conditions left undetermined by physiology, without interfering in its laws. Though rooted in the body the mind is free in its actions from bodily determination. Mind and body cannot be treated, therefore, as two aspects of the same thing, for then the mind could not do anything but what the bodily mechanism determines. Polanyi refers to his view as 'the viable core of the traditional mind-body dualism'. Mind and body interact according to the logic of tacit knowing.

objectivism – According to Polanyi 'the false ideal of objectivity' in science as pure exteriority in knowledge, based on a detachment of subjectivity from objectivity, and seeking to establish absolutely dispassionate, impersonal knowledge by eliminating the personal coefficient and thereby relieving us from the responsibility of holding beliefs or making personal judgments. Polanyi argues that this amounts to an absurd mechanisation of knowledge. While personal knowledge implies an 'ontology of mind', objectivism implies a 'mindless knower' – i.e. the fallacy of excluding the knowing subject from the field of knowledge, which Schrödinger called the 'exclusion principle'.

objectivity – the establishing of cognitive contact with reality independent of our perceiving or conceiving of it and the submission of our minds to its compelling universal claims upon them; the conformity of knowledge to a rationality in nature, deeper than our understanding of it, the reality of which is manifested in the indeterminate scope of its true implications far beyond the range of our experience of it. Objectivity in this sense implies the unity of form and being or of the theoretical and empirical components in reality, which we cannot know except through penetrating into its inner intelligibility and letting our minds fall under its compelling force.

ontology – the doctrine of being or of what really exists, the objective reality to which our thought refers and which gives it meaning. There are different ontological levels, or levels of existence; the higher levels, comprising the least tangible things, have the 'deepest reality'. There is thus an ontology of mind as a higher form of being. Of special significance for Polanyi's concept of science is a structural kinship between the knowing mind and the objective reality of being which it knows. This is the ontological import of tacit knowing which undergirds all explicit scientific operations. At this point Polanyi's conception of science differs radically from that of the positivists for whom scientific theories are no more than convenient economic arrangements of our observations, with no claim to bearing upon being.

personal knowledge – the responsible participation of the person as an active rational centre of consciousness in all acts of understanding and knowing. It is only a person who can think, mean, interpret, understand; only a person who can appraise the validity of an argument or exercise a judgment in relating evidence to an external reality which he seeks to apprehend; only a person who can discern a coherent pattern in nature and use it as a clue in active pursuit of his inquiry; only a person who can submit his mind to the compelling demands of reality upon him; only a person who can think and decide as he must under obligation to the truth; and only a person who can act responsibly with universal intent in his knowing. All this does not mean that personal knowledge is subjective, for the personal participation of the knower is controlled by impersonal requirements and submission to universal standards which transcend his subjectivity. It is only a person who is capable of distinguishing what he knows from his knowing of it, or objective states of affairs from his own subjective fantasies, and only a person, therefore, who can engage in authentically objective operations. Personal knowledge is a way of knowing through responsible commitment to the claims of reality in which the personal and the objective are fused together in the act of establishing contact with reality and its intrinsic rationality. In personal knowledge responsibility and truth are two complementary aspects of commitment to reality:

the act of judgment is the personal pole and the independent reality on which it bears is its external pole.

phenomenalism – a way of knowing in which we abstract the appearance of things or their phenomenal surface from the actual ground on which they rest and reduce our knowledge to sense data alone. This gives rise to an insoluble problem, for there is no way within appearances to test their validity or to refer beyond them to the outside world. The dualism upon which phenomenalism reposes has the effect of cutting off form from being, or structure from reality, so that the phenomenal patterns uprooted from their controlling ground fragment into separate particulars, and some form of external organisation and mechanical connection must be imposed on them to replace the spontaneous integration or organisation they have in nature. Polanyi's theory of knowledge aims at restoring the unity of knowing and being in the ontological sub-structure of knowledge, which cuts behind false abstraction and its disintegrating processes.

positivism – the view which denies that we can know more than tangible external facts. It seeks to purify science from metaphysics by avoiding any ontological reference of knowledge to reality, and aims at the achievement of strict detachment and impersonality by discarding all unprovable beliefs as arbitrary personal manifestations. According to the positivist view of knowledge scientific theories must not go beyond sense experience by affirming anything that cannot be experimentally observed or tested, so that whenever an empirical observation turns up that conflicts with it, a theory is deemed to be falsified and must be dropped immediately. Scientific theories are ultimately only useful mental constructs or sets of useful conventions for the handling of observational data, or devices like maps, time-tables or telephone directories with reference to which we may record events and compute their future course in our observations. Theories of this kind deny any claim to inherent rationality, so that, as Polanyi argues, they lack any real persuasive power. In common with empiricism and phenomenalism, positivism offers a complete mechanico-causal interpretation of man and human affairs which disintegrates all rational grounds for human convictions and actions. Moreover, it offers a mechanistic account of the human mind, in identifying the mind with the physiological mechanism of the brain, and thereby denatures man and denies him any capacity for independent thought.

premiss – the premisses in any logical argument are the basic statements or assumptions from which the conclusion is deduced and on which it is claimed finally to rely. The premisses of science are the ulitmate suppositions or beliefs about the general nature of things in the universe on which all scientific activity in research, theory or teaching relies. The premisses of science cannot be explicitly formulated, and can be found authentically manifested only in the practice of science, and as maintained in the tradition of science. As such they are never affirmed as presuppositions of science by themselves, for they are reciprocally related to the deepening of knowledge and are subject to continuous modification and establishment as under their guidance new facts are discovered and actual knowledge is advanced.

proximal/distal – two terms of tacit knowledge in which we rely on our awareness of one term (the proximal) in order to attend to another (the distal). Thus we use our own body, without being explicitly aware of it, in order to attend to things beyond ourselves. We rely on our spectacles, to which we pay no attention, in order to see things through them. Proximal/distal thus correspond to the pair of terms *subsidiary/focal*.

rationalism – the view that man must be free to follow the natural light of the reason alone in the knowledge of all that exists, and that everything (at least in principle) is explainable by being reduced through deductive reasoning into a single comprehensive system of thought. Since rationalism admits only demonstrable knowledge, it calls in question all authority and rejects all belief as unfounded prejudice. Polanyi objects that a consistent rationalism is nonsensical, for no rational argument can operate without informal or indefinable factors either in relating thought to being or in applying the rules governing a logico-deductive system – hence no argument can operate rationally outside a framework of fundamental beliefs. Polanyi also insists that no human mind can function without accepting authority, custom and tradition, for it must rely on them even for the use of language, but also for the continuance and preservation of human institutions, not least the institution he calls 'the republic of science'.

reality – not directly definable, but may be defined indirectly with respect to the universal constraint to which human knowing must submit if it is to be true or accepted as valid. Instead of operating with the traditional distinction between appearance and reality which implies a false dichotomy between knowing and being, Polanyi defines reality in respect of the unlimited capacity of things for revealing themselves to our inquiries in yet unthought of, or quite unexpected, ways in the future, thus manifesting a domain of independent being with inherent significance or rationality that is not exhausted by our conceptions of it and does not depend on our knowing for its truth and existence. Regarded in this way, minds possess a 'deeper reality' than cobblestones, although cobblestones are 'more real' in the sense of being tangible. Science is committed to the belief in an independent reality over which we have no control and whose compelling claims over us we cannot rationally avoid. It is by reference to the claims of reality that our acts of knowledge are kept within the bounds of rational objectivity and are justified, and thereby have the force of universal law behind them.

reductionism – the belief that everything can be explained by recourse to a single simpler principle, or that all knowledge can be reduced to a single level of explanatory connections. More generally, reductionism is the fallacy of redefining one set of entities and their relations in terms of a more limited set of entities and their relations, instead of treating the latter as a limiting case of the former. Reductionist thought, for example, claims that in biology evolution and all animal behaviour can be explained in terms of causal mechanisms and ultimately in terms of the laws of physics and chemistry; and that, likewise, all human life and behaviour can be interpreted by redefining them in terms of the behaviour of more limited animate or inanimate entities and the laws governing their organisation. Polanyi argues not only that this inverts the structure of science (e.g. of Newtonian physics as a limiting case of relativistic physics) but that reductionism is destructive of all essential and distinctive features in nature, especially in its richer or more complex manifestations. He opposes reductionism by setting against it an alternative explanation which is its precise opposite. For example, within an organism instead of the higher level of operational principles being explained in terms of the lower, the lower falls significantly under the control of the higher where it is left open to it through its boundary conditions. While the higher principles rely on the operations of the lower they are not accountable in terms of them. Reductionism 'downward' is thus opposed by a sublimation 'upward' from the lower to the higher levels of reality and meaning.

tacit *dimension* — the unaccountable, inarticulate component in perception and knowledge, a basic unreflecting awareness of things is quite different from the clear-cut awareness we have when focussing our attention directly on them. We always know more than we can tell. It is on this deep subsidiary awareness that all skills, explicit thought, formal reasoning, and articulate knowing and communication rely. Even the most completely formalised knowledge (e.g. through logic or mathematics) must include informal or tacit coefficients, for it is only by relying on them that formal systems can operate meaningfully. This is evident in the bearing of thought and speech upon some reality or the bearing of some skill upon an intended end; and also in the way our minds spontaneously integrate particulars into significant wholes, as in the recognition of a physiognomy, or integrate clues into a focal target, as in scientific intuition and discovery. Tacit knowing, Polanyi claims, is the fundamental power of the mind which creates explicit knowing and lends meaning to and controls its use. Tacit knowledge and explicit knowledge are opposed to one another but they are not sharply divided. While tacit knowledge can be possessed by itself, explicit knowledge must rely on being tacitly understood and applied. Hence all knowledge is either tacit or rooted in tacit knowledge. A wholly explicit knowledge is unthinkable. This tacit dimension provides the unifying ground of all knowledge, rooting it in the concrete situations of life and society in the world; and as such provides the continuous epistemological field which integrates the sciences and the arts and does away with the age-old dualisms which have led to the fragmentation of human culture.

scientism — a generalised form of reductionism, in accordance with which knowledge of things at all levels is reductively redefined in terms of a limited, objectivist and mechanist understanding of nature. According to Polanyi, scientism which disposes of all beliefs and traditionally guiding ideas has cruelly fettered the human spirit, for it destroys the creative symbiosis between science, faith and society.

semantics — the theory of meaning in language or other symbolic systems, or the study of signs and their relations to the realities they signify. In contrast to syntactics, which has to do with the relations of linguistic or symbolic terms to one another, semantics has to do with their objective or ontological reference beyond themselves. Since all meaning tends to be displaced away from ourselves, Polanyi seeks to elucidate the semantic aspect of knowing both in its tacit and in its explicit forms. Since tacit knowing provides the informal infrastructure on which all knowing relies, he is especially concerned to clarify the function of the semantic aspect or ontological reference of tacit knowing under the direction (or 'vectorial' power) of which explicit knowledge is guided toward its objective, e.g. in the way we are tacitly aware of clues in their bearing upon some hidden reality which as such can yet reveal itself in an indeterminate range of future discoveries. In the hierarchical structure of reality, as Polanyi envisages it, the meaning of the higher level cannot be accounted for by reductive analysis to the elements forming the lower levels: in this event semantics has to do with the cross-level references only 'upward' and never 'downward'.

transcendence — extension beyond the bounds of the world, of human experience or comprehension. Traditionally, transcendence *over* the world is applied to God who is independent of the universe he has made and who while everywhere present in it cannot be regarded as contained within its space-time dimensions or as controlled within the limits of finite knowledge. God may be apprehended, but not comprehended, for he is infinitely greater than we can conceive: he transcends all our thought and speech about him. Transcendence *in* the world is applied to realities that are independent of our knowledge of them, that can be known only out of themselves but which cannot be confined within the limits of our descriptions. In Polanyi's thought transcendence is applied in various related ways. Belief in the transcendent is belief in reality beyond ourselves which presses for realisation in our minds but which is expected to reveal itself indeterminately in the future. It is in submission to the transcendent or spiritual reality of truth over which we have no control, in acknowledgment of transcendent obligations and in the dedication to transcendent ideals which we affirm with universal intent, that we have our freedom as rational beings. In Polanyi's conception of the nature of the universe as an expanding horizon of hierarchical levels with their boundary conditions, each level is transcended by one more intangible and more meaningful than it, so that the most intangible things are the most real and the most transcendent. The range of reality everywhere exceeds our most complete grasp, but it beckons us forward in the promise of revealing ever new truths. That is transcendence *in* the world, which is not to be confused with the transcendence of God *over* the world, to whom the world as a whole is left open or indeterminate at its boundary conditions: thus transcendence in the world opens out toward and points to the transcendence of God over the world.

universal intent – the expression Polanyi uses to describe the responsible decision of the scientist as he stands under the judgment of the hidden reality he seeks to uncover. While his acts of anticipatory discernment, inquiry and discovery are intensely personal, they are not self-willed or arbitrary, for from beginning to end the scientist acts under obligation to an external objective and submits to the impersonal requirements or truth-claims of reality upon him. In acknowledging the jurisdiction of this reality over him the scientist submits to it in good conscience as universally valid, and correspondingly claims universal validity for what he must think and say of it in accordance with its legislation, and expects that others who share with him the same commitment to reality will recognise and accept its universal validity as well, and indeed ought to do so. This is not so say that he thereby establishes universality for his results, for as a scientist he cannot know that his claims will be universally accepted. All he can do is to put forward his claims with universal intent, that is, to claim universal validity for his results under the obligatory character of the fundamental nature of reality which in fidelity to the truth he can do no other than acknowledge, and to the compelling demands of which he responds through an act of self-imposed obligation to the same universal standards of validity. In the last resort it is reality itself that must be the judge of the truth or falsity of his work, but the scientist accepts that judgment as his own in a responsible act of binding self-legislation – hence the standards he sets for himself in his scientific activity are the standards imposed by objective reality itself on all scientists.

NOTES ON AUTHORS

The Rev. Dr John Barr, mechanical engineer and theologian, is a minister of the Church of Scotland formerly Kilmacolm, Renfrewshire.

The Rev. Peter Forster, chemist and theologian, priest of the Church of England in Liverpool, is engaged in research at the University of Edinburgh.

The Rev. Dr Colin E. Gunton, a minister of the United Reformed Church in England, is a lecturer in the Department of Theology, King's College, University of London.

The Rev. Daniel W. Hardy, priest of the Church of England, formerly of the University of Oxford, is a lecturer in the Department of Theology, University of Birmingham.

Mr Arthur Walter James, distinguished Journalist and Editor, formerly on the staff of the Manchester Guardian, Editor of The Times Educational Supplement, and Reader in Journalism, University of Canterbury, New Zealand, is Principal of St. Catherine's, Cumberland Lodge, Great Windsor Park.

The Rev. John C. Puddefoot, mathematician and theologian, is a priest of the Church of England, in Darlington, County Durham.

The Very Rev. Thomas F. Torrance is Emeritus Professor of Christian Dogmatics, University of Edinburgh, and former Moderator of the General Assembly of the Church of Scotland. He is Michael Polanyi's Literary Executor.

INDEX OF NAMES